A PLAY BY

DAVE ARMSTRONG

AND

OSCAR KIGHTLEY

NELSON
CENGAGE Learning™

Australia • Brazil • Japan • Korea • Mexico • Singapore • Spain • United Kingdom • United States

Niu Sila
1st Edition
Dave Armstrong
Oscar Kightley

Cover illustration & design: Brenda Cantell
Back cover photo: Scott Venning with kind assistance from the Arts Foundation
Reprint: Jess Lovell

Acknowledgements
The authors and publishers wish to thank Jenny Thomas for writing the English Activities and Jaclyn Druitt for the drama activities which support *Niu Sila* in this publication.

For product information and technology assistance,
in Australia call **1300 790 853**;
in New Zealand call **0800 449 725**

For permission to use material from this text or product, please email
aust.permissions@cengage.com

National Library of New Zealand Cataloguing-in-Publication Data
Armstrong, Dave, 1961 -
Niu Sila / Dave Armstrong and Oscar Kightley.

ISBN 978 0 17 095033 6

1. Samoans-New Zealand-Juvenile drama. 2. New Zealand-Race relations-Juvenile drama. [1. Samoans-New Zealand-Drama. 2. Plays. 3. New Zealand-Race relations-Drama.]
I. Kightley, Oscar. II. Title.

NZ822.3-dc 22

Cengage Learning Australia
Level 7, 80 Dorcas Street
South Melbourne, Victoria Australia 3205

Cengage Learning New Zealand
Unit 4B Rosedale Office Park
331 Rosedale Road, Albany, North Shore 0632, NZ

For learning solutions, visit **cengage.co.nz**

Printed in Australia by Ligare Pty Limited.
6 7 8 9 10 11 12 19 18 17 16 15

Contents

Niu Sila – from the beginning

SOMETIME AROUND ABOUT 1997: Dave Armstrong and Oscar Kightley were both working on a television sketch show in Wellington called *Skitz*. Dave, who grew up in Wellington next door to a Pacific Island family, mentioned to Oscar that he was thinking of writing a play about two friends, one Pacific Islander; one Palagi, who grew up next to each other.

Dave asked Oscar if he would like to write the play with him. Oscar, who grew up in Te Atatu in Auckland and had many of his own stories about growing up next to Palagi neighbours, agreed. They applied for a Creative New Zealand grant and *Niu Sila* was born.

About a year later, the boys had spent their grant money, but still hadn't written the play! Dave flew to Auckland, where Oscar was now living, with a bunch of notes and the two spent a very busy weekend together. By the time Dave flew back to Wellington a few days later, most of the play was written.

Later on, scenes were rewritten and an ending was tagged on, and the first draft of the script was ready. A private reading with Dave Fane and Damon Andrews was organised at Dave's place and everyone present (five people) agreed that there was a good play in there.

CUT TO FIVE YEARS LATER: Dave submitted the play to the Adam Playreading Series where it got its first 'professional' reading. The day after the Adam Playreading, two professional theatres programmed the play. The play was rewritten after a couple of workshops, and opened at Downstage Theatre in March 2004. *Niu Sila* has now been performed in Auckland, Wellington, and Christchurch as well as many festivals throughout the country. It has also toured to England and won several awards.

From the beginning, both Oscar and Dave agreed that just two actors – one white and one brown – would play all the many parts. This meant it could tour to schools and festivals easily. There would be no props, a simple set and basic costumes. How would the audience know which character was which? Thanks to two fantastic actors, Damon Andrews and Dave Fane, and a great director, Conrad Newport, who staged the play with just two chairs as props, it never seemed to be a problem.

More recently, the play has been performed by school groups with a large cast, and it works just as well. The main point of the play is the story, rather than how it is performed.

So that's how *Niu Sila* got started. If it wasn't for the generous financial support of Creative New Zealand, who fund all sorts of exciting things in the arts in New Zealand, *Niu Sila* may never have got written. If it wasn't for the generosity of Denis and Verna Adam and their Adam Playreading Series, the play may never have found its way to professional theatres. And if it wasn't for Creative New Zealand, the play certainly would not ha overseas for people in countries to see it.

Helping hands

Throughout the process of producing *Niu Sila* Dave and Oscar were helped by several key organisations that any budding young playwright or performer should be aware of.

Adam Playreading

The Adam Foundation was established in 1975 by Denis Adam and his wife Verna.

Following an extensive career as an Insurance broker, Denis Adam currently maintains an office in Wellington for Adam Consultants & Administrators and The Adam Foundation.

The Adam Foundation is a passionate supporter of Music and Art in New Zealand, reflecting Denis and Verna's strong interest in both disciplines.

The Adam Playreading Series is now in its eleventh year in Wellington at Downstage Theatre. It provides rehearsed readings of four full-length New Zealand plays ready to be considered for professional production, and yet to be produced in Wellington.

This is an ideal opportunity for playwrights to receive professional presentations of their full-length work at close to final draft stage. Many plays have been picked up for production as a result of this series.

Niu Sila was commissioned by Creative New Zealand in 1997. Armstrong and Kightley completed a draft script soon after, but various commitments for both of them meant that the play had never been performed. However, in 2003, the writers submitted the play to the Adam Playreading selection committee. The play was accepted, actors Fane and Andrews contacted, and Director Conrad Newport was brought in. During the weekend of the playreading, the script was workshopped, and a highly successful Adam Playreading followed. The day after the reading, *Niu Sila* was invited to be part of the 2004 Downstage Programme.

'The Adam Playreading Series was crucial to the development of *Niu Sila*,' says Oscar Kightley, whose previous play *Dawn Raids* had also received an Adam Playreading. 'We had a script, but we had never seen it performed or had the chance to workshop it.'

'It was amazing to see the effect *Niu Sila* had on a live audience,' says Dave Armstrong, 'even at the playreading stage. Afterwards we knew we had a play that was capable of really affecting people.'

'The feedback session afterwards was also fantastic,' says Kightley, 'some really helpful comments were made. We're both very grateful to Denis for his support of theatre through the Adam Playreadings.'

Creative New Zealand

Creative New Zealand is New Zealand's main arts development agency. Its role is to promote the arts of New Zealand, support artists and encourage more New Zealanders to enjoy the arts. It does this by funding a wide range of projects by artists and arts organisations, advocating for the arts and undertaking initiatives and research projects.

They fund projects that:

- focus on the development of New Zealand arts and artists
- are stand-alone arts activities with a start and an end point, or are programmes of work over a clearly defined period of time.

Creative New Zealand has a limited amount of money to spread across its wide range of activities. Project funding is just one of a number of programmes they operate every year. The amount of money available for project funding is limited ($7.45 million in the previous financial year).

Project funding is a competitive process. In general, less than one in three applications is offered a grant.

Creative New Zealand also offers a range of awards, bursaries, scholarships, fellowships and residencies.

Writing *Niu Sila*

Below **Dave Armstrong** and **Oscar Kightley** talk about the process of writing *Niu Sila*. We thought it might be interesting for you to see that the idea of drafting, editing and rewriting isn't just something teachers make you do to annoy you. Rather it is a process inherent in all published products.

What got you into writing, specifically the art of playwriting?

Dave: I've always loved plays. Initially I was a musician but ended up writing bits of shows I played the trumpet in.

Oscar: I enjoyed performing and visualising a well-written scene in my head. Being the writer of plays, you get to see it as an audience member and relive the moment of creation.

How did you two meet?

Dave: I think we met when I was working on TV3's *Skitz*. I went to Oscar's play *Fresh off the Boat* and was very impressed. We had a meeting at a bad Turkish café in Hataitai in Wellington. Once Oscar started working on *Skitz* we saw more of each other, we even played in a soccer team together a couple to times until Oscar collapsed from exhaustion.

Have you collaborated on work before?

Dave: We worked together a lot on *Skitz* – little sketches rather than a whole play.

Oscar: It was here (at *Skitz*) that Dave had an idea for *Niu Sila*, based on an episode in his life, of living next to a family from a different culture and becoming friends. I mean, when you think about it, everyone's got a mate like that. You may not necessarily keep in contact, but the experience stays with you.

What inspired you both to write a play that spanned over three decades?

Dave: Most of *Niu Sila* was written about seven years ago. Oscar and I were in our thirties (well I was anyway, Os was late twenties) when we wrote the story. Lots of it is autobiographical so I guess if we left it till we were seventy we would have written a play spanning seven decades.

Oscar: It was the obvious form, really. Stylistically, the changes are easier to facilitate in a play (and cheaper) than say, a TV series or a film. As far as the thrust of the story is concerned, it's easier to be a mate with someone when you're five than when you're twenty-five.

Considering you both live in different cities, how did you find the process of collaboration?

Oscar: Well, trans-city collaboration isn't as hard as you think.

Dave: I did some preparatory stuff and wrote a lot of notes in novel form based on my early life living next to a PI family in Wellington. I flew up to Auckland with the aid of a Creative NZ grant, and Oscar and I spent the weekend 'dramatizing' what I had written then writing scenes of our own…

Oscar: We workshopped and wrote pretty much day and night.

Dave: We almost had a finished draft. We edited each other's work then basically had a working draft. I did a bit of editing after that then it was ready to have its first workshop (June 2003).

Oscar: Having the internet and cheap airfares definitely helped the collaborative process.

What was it like to work on an intimate project, such as a play?

Dave: It was real fun. Working with Os (and also the Nakeds I've later discovered) is different from working with other writers. 'The work' as in the play, sits on the computer and you have a turn at writing it, maybe talking to your co-writer, maybe not. Then you go and eat or go for a walk and happily let the other guy write a scene. Dare I say it it's more of a relaxed 'Polynesian' style of writing than two uptight Palagis arguing over every syllable.

Oscar: It was cool, I mean it, the best thing in the world. What really excites me about a play is the immediacy.

How did your actors contribute in the writing process?

Oscar: They didn't. We wrote the script. In rehearsals, the actors brought their ideas but ultimately…we wrote the dialogue and pieced the scenes together to form a story.

Dave: We had two two-day workshops before rehearsals started and I spent the first week sitting in rehearsals making changes. Both actors contributed to the script in different ways. Damon was really helpful in making the last scene believable, he kept saying, 'my character's too much of a wimp' and we changed quite a lot of that last scene based on improvisations he and Dave did. Dave Fane is a brilliant comic so he added lots of funny stuff that we gladly accepted. (He also added stuff we didn't, for various reasons including taste!) I find actors love it if the writers are flexible and will use their ideas. However, I also think you have to put your foot down occasionally and say 'No Fane, Mrs Tafioka would NOT say 'hot tamale'!

Would you credit their offerings?

Oscar: No. All plays get workshopped. The actors contribute but the initial inspiration to form a play out of their ideas, experiences and memories remain the writers' own. I mean, if we as writers credit the actors, where does it end? Keeping it simple is paramount.

Dave: This is a tricky area. You turn up with a complete script, as we did with *Niu Sila*, then an actor improvises a line or changes it slightly, then suddenly you think, should I credit them as a writer? I don't agree with that. As well as creating a minefield with credit, it involves financial problems. It would be different if an actor turned up with a whole scene they had written, but that didn't happen.

During workshopping many scenes were 'tweaked' and one or two scenes were extensively rewritten, and improvisations were carried out in the all-important last scene in the TAB which had heaps of rewrites. Some scenes hardly changed at all from pen to performance.

Having said all that, *Niu Sila* would not have been the play it was were it not for the incredible contribution to the script process made by the director Conrad Newport, who is an excellent actor and writer himself, and the two actors.

What inspires you to write?

Oscar: I guess the joy of telling a story and the joy of hearing one told. It's such an unbelievable feeling. Stories are great.

Dave: Real life.

This interview is included in the Auckland Theatre Company teacher's pack which supported their 2005 season of *Niu Sila*. The interview was conducted by Louise Tu'u and edited by Lynne Cardy. The full teacher's pack is available to download from the Auckland Theatre Company website: www.atc.co.nz/EducationUnit/

The staging of *Niu Sila*

When *Niu Sila* was first written, it was intended to be a 'two-hander'. All the characters in the script were to be performed by only two actors – one Pacific Island male and one Palagi (white) male. The script was written in such a way that as the actors changed character, they always talked to a character played by the other actor, not to 'themselves.'

For example, when Mrs Burton (played by the Palagi actor) is at home with her husband, Mr Burton (played by the Pacific Island actor), the couple engage in dialogue and argue etc. However, when Peter Burton is there (also played by the Palagi actor) he never talks directly to his mother as he does to his father.

There are no scenes between Mrs Burton and Peter (both played by the Palagi actor) or Sulu and Ioane (both played by the Pacific Island actor). When two characters played by one actor (e.g. Peter and Mrs Burton) are in the same scene (such as at the beginning when Ioane turns up to take Peter to school) the Palagi actor 'changes' from playing Peter to playing Mrs Burton while Ioane is talking.

Despite this play originally being a two-hander, it is obvious when you see the array of colourful characters, that it can be also performed by large casts and with extras, which makes it an ideal play for a class.

Oscar Kightley and Dave Armstrong

Cast

Characters (in order of appearance)

PETER BURTON	A Palagi boy (aged from 5 to about 30 over the course of the play).
IOANE TAFIOKA	A Pacific Island boy who lives next door to Peter (aged from 5 to about 30 over the course of the play).
DAD (Frank Burton)	Peter's father. A Palagi university lecturer in his forties.
MUM (Margaret Burton)	Peter's mother. A Palagi housewife in her late thirties.
VERONICA	A young Palagi girl in Ioane's class, about 5 years old.
STEPHANIE	A young Palagi girl in Ioane's class, about 5 years old.
ANDREA	A young Palagi girl in Ioane's class, about 5 years old.
LORRAINE	A young Palagi girl in Ioane's class, about 5 years old.
MISS H (Miss Hagan)	A very strict, racist Pakeha schoolteacher in her 30s or 40s.
Mr T (Mr Tafioka)	Ioane's father. A tall, strong, silent and smiling Pacific Island man, aged about 35.
MRS T (Mrs Tafioka)	Ioane's mother. A warm yet very bossy Pacific Island woman, aged about 35.
MRS H (Mrs Heathcote)	A nosy and disapproving Palagi next-door neighbour in her 60s.
CRIMINAL	A large, overweight and slightly pompous Pacific Island minister in his 40s.
UNCLE POU	An often drunk Pacific Island man in his 30s.
SULU	Ioane's younger sister (aged from 4 to about 15 over the course of the play).
MR PATEL	A friendly local diary owner and a cricket player in his 40s. Has a strong Indian accent.
MR PATEL JUNIOR	Mr Patel's son.
COP	An aggressive and unfriendly Palagi policeman in his 30s.
LISA	An attractive and friendly Pakeha girl aged about 15.
COURT OFFICIAL	A male or female official in their 30s or 40s.
JUDGE	An older man in his 50s or 60s. Though strict, he is fair and tolerant.
TAMATI	A Maori boy about 15. A bit of a lad and very interested in girls.
NUN	A very friendly and slightly doddery Palagi nun in her 70s.
BOY (Vincent)	A six-year old Chinese boy from Hong Kong. He speaks with a strong Chinese accent and is quite impatient.
EXTRAS in the TAB	A bunch of mainly men sitting around, watching television and placing bets.
EXTRAS in the church	A large number of Pacific Islanders singing.
EXTRAS in school	Children in Ioane and Peter's class.

Peter, a young Palagi boy, and Ioane, a young Pacific Islander, nervously enter and sing a Pacific song and do the actions.

PETER and IOANE:

Ko e kufani
Ko e manu iloilo
Kua sia e ia hana fata
Ke hele aki a pepe
Kua koli goagoa a pepe
He vihi hana hui
O fakalofa lahi a koe ma pepe
Kua samusamu he kufani

They lose their way and start laughing as they sing.

PETER and IOANE: Inky pinky ponky

IOANE and PETER: What?

Peter, an adult, is in a TAB. The environment is obviously a foreign one for him, and he surveys the scene with some amusement – an interested tourist mixing with the locals.

PETER: I don't usually gamble, but it was Melbourne Cup Day. I thought I'd have a bit of fun. The staff had made a special effort: free beer, nibbles, little cardboard hats, and there were women there, and men in suits. Not your normal sleazy TAB atmosphere. Everyone was talking about the big race. Well, almost everyone. Tucked away in the corner was a small group of Pacific Island men, watching some obscure trotting race in the South Island. All smoking; none laughing. I didn't notice him at first.

We see Ioane Tafioka as an adult. He notices Peter and considers ignoring him, but it's too late. Peter isn't sure how to approach him, it's been so long.

PETER: Ioane.

Ioane isn't pleased to see Peter.

IOANE: Peter.

PETER: How are you?

IOANE: All right.

PETER: Must be over twenty years.

IOANE: Didn't think you'd be into this.

PETER: I'm not really. But you know. Melbourne Cup and all that. Half the office are here. You good?

IOANE: Yeah, I just said. All right?

PETER: Where have you been hiding?

IOANE: Haven't been hiding. Went back to the island.

PETER: Yeah I'd heard that. Great.

IOANE: Why'd you ask then?

PETER: Just wanted to know how you've been. Remember you always talked about going back?

IOANE: No.

PETER: Only every day. We should catch up. Here's my numbers.

Peter hands over a card.

IOANE: *(reading)* 'Bicultural Policy Analyst, Ministry of Pacific Island Affairs.'

PETER: Pays the bills. Still fishing?

IOANE: What do you think?

A pause.

IOANE: I gotta place this bet.

Ioane tries to lose Peter, but Peter follows him.

PETER: Yeah, we were thinking about a flutter on *Jonah's Wife*. Thirty bucks a win, what do you think?

IOANE: Donkey. *(to the TAB attendant)* Two dollars each way on number 5 and a dollar quinella on 5 and 8.

Peter tries another tack.

PETER: So, how's the family?

IOANE: Good.

PETER: Your mother good?

IOANE: Okay.

PETER: My Mum still talks about her. And your Dad?

IOANE: Alive.

PETER: Are they still living out at Mangere?

IOANE: No, they've got a villa in Remuera.

PETER: Really?

Peter realises Ioane is joking.

IOANE: I better get going.

PETER: I thought you were waiting for your race?

IOANE: Gotta do stuff.

PETER: You can't go yet.

IOANE: Why not?

PETER: You should come to dinner some time. We could catch up.

IOANE: We've caught up.

PETER: You know what I mean. *(pause)* Look, you're not still pissed off about ...

IOANE: Course not. I'm just busy, right?

PETER: Then how about a beer sometime? My shout.

IOANE: What? You think I can't afford a beer?

PETER: What's your problem bro?

IOANE: I'm not your bro.

PETER: Okay okay, fine … sorry to bother you. I'll get going.

IOANE: Fine by me.

PETER: *(angry)* See you later then. Maybe in another twenty years.

IOANE: Fine by me.

Peter eyeballs Ioane.

PETER: Good!

Ioane eyeballs him back.

IOANE: Great!

Ioane goes back to his race, leaving an angry Peter.

PETER: That was my 'best friend' Ioane Tafioka. He was nothing like the little kid that first knocked on my door over twenty years ago.

We hear music from about 25 years ago. Peter Burton, aged 5, squats down.

PETER: Daaaaaddddd, Dad.

DAD: What is it, Peter?

PETER: Can you come and wipe my bottom?

DAD: Do it yourself, you're five years old.

PETER: No, I want you to.

DAD: For God's sake.

Ioane, aged five, barges in.

IOANE: Hello.

MUM: Hello.

IOANE: Is Peter in, Miss Burton? I've come to take him to school.

MUM: Certainly – he won't be long. And what's your name?

IOANE: Ioane Tafioka, Miss.

MUM: Nice to meet you Ioane. *(calling out)* Peter, you've got a visitor.

IOANE: Hey Peter.

PETER: Ioane? What are you doing here?

IOANE: I'm walking with you to school 'cos you're my friend.

Ioane puts his arm around Peter. Peter squirms.

PETER: Friend? Just 'cos I picked him in my cricket team a couple of days ago. Michael Taylor had a bike with monkey bars and a banana seat. Now there was a friend.

IOANE: You got a nice house, Peter.

MUM: That's a lovely thing to say, Ioane. And where do you live?

IOANE: 23 Otahu Street, Miss Burton.

MUM: Oh. That's by the … um …

IOANE: The reservation.

MUM: Peter's father and I don't like to call it that. It's by the McKinlay Reserve isn't it?

IOANE: That's right. The reservation. 'Cos that's where all the dark people live. Like me! Ha, ha, ha.

Ioane whoops like a red-Indian.

IOANE: Woh woh woh woh woh!

He pretends to shoot arrows.

IOANE: Peow! Peow!

MUM: A long time ago, the, ah, 'reservation' was considered the best part of town.

IOANE: It still is. 'Cos we live there. Come on Peter, we go to school.

MUM: Don't forget your sandwiches, Peter. And take *one* piece of fruit. Would you like an apple, Ioane?

Too late – he's already taken one.

IOANE: Fank you Miss Burton.

MUM: And don't forget your handkerchief for Miss Hagan, Peter. She'll keep you in if you forget.

IOANE: Bye Miss Burton.

PETER: You've told me twice already, Mum. Now don't bloody nag.

Ioane is horrified.

IOANE: Peter. You can't talk to your mother like that.

PETER: Why not? Dad does.

IOANE: But she's your mother. You better be careful Peter, *(whispering)* you'll get a whack.

PETER: Nah, it's okay. They don't believe in hitting.

IOANE: That's crazy, man. You should never speak to your mother like that, Peter. Say sorry.

PETER: Don't be stupid.

IOANE: Say sorry!

PETER: Sorry Mum.

IOANE: That's better.

MUM: Apology accepted, Peter. Nice to meet you, Ioane.

IOANE: Nice to meet you, Miss Burton. See you.

They start to walk to school.

PETER: Where's your lunch?

IOANE: I buy my lunch today, my mother give me a dollar.

PETER: Does your mother give you a dollar every day?

IOANE: Only when she win the race. If she loses, she give me a whack.

PETER: I got 50 cents when I helped Billy Walker do his paper run.

IOANE: You buy lollies?

PETER: My parents made me bank it in my Post Office Account.

IOANE: Mum says next time she win the double at Trentham, she buy a TV.

PETER: Even Michael Taylor doesn't have a TV.

IOANE: You must have one?

PETER: No way.

IOANE: But you rich.

PETER: Dad doesn't like the noise.

IOANE: But that's why you buy a TV, stupid, to watch the picture and listen to the noise!

PETER: Not my father.

IOANE: My father love the TV. He say it's the best thing about living in Niu Sila.

PETER: Dad says books and the radio are better for us.

IOANE: Then your Dad bloody stupid.

They both laugh.

IOANE: My uncle got a TV. We go to his place on Friday night to watch the *Wacky Races* and a cowboy movie. You see the *Wacky Races*?

PETER: Yeah, it's cool.

IOANE: Race you to the dairy.

PETER: Okay, I'm Dick Dastardly and you're the Caveman.

IOANE: No, I'm Anthill Mob and you're Penelope Pittstop. No, you're Peter Pittstop.

PETER: Ioane and I walked to school together every day – rain or shine. It only took five minutes to get to school but we made it last thirty. Mum worried, but Dad heartily approved of our dawdling.

DAD: Calm down, Marg. Playing in the gutter is the best education a kid can have. You know why? 'Cos there's no adults around to muck them up.

MARG: Come on Frank, that's going a bit far.

DAD: What a child learns in that sacred half-hour is priceless – can't be taught in any book.

PETER: Dad may have been right about the 'sacred half-hour', though I suspect the real reason for his theory was that he couldn't be bothered giving us a lift to school.

IOANE: Psst Peter. Got any lunch money?

PETER: No, but you can share my tomato sandwiches.

IOANE: No thanks.

PETER: Didn't your mother win the race?

IOANE: Yeah, but she had to pay the phone bill before it get cut off. Let's play on the jungle gym.

PETER: I think we should finish chewing first. Mum says you can choke.

IOANE: Come on Peter, it's fun.

PETER: I tried to make it across, but my palms would sting after two rungs, then I'd drop down onto the asphalt, jarring my feet. But not Ioane. He could cross three or four times, no problem.

Ioane moves from bar to bar no problem.

PETER: *(to Ioane)* Ioane, you're a bloody monkey.

IOANE: Come on Peter. You try!

PETER: I'm not allowed. Mum says they should put soft padding underneath.

IOANE: Come on man. It's really easy.

PETER: *(to audience)* Then I noticed a long pony-tail hanging down from his head. I'd never seen it before; he must have hidden it. *(to Ioane)* Hey Ioane, what's that thing hanging down?

IOANE: That's my dick!

Ioane and Peter laugh uncontrollably.

PETER: No, from your head.

IOANE: It's special. They cut it off when I'm about 12 and all my aunties and uncles give me money – even the minister.

PETER: How much?

IOANE: Two dollar; five dollar. When my brother Alana had his cut off, Uncle Pou give him twenty dollar.

PETER: That's it. I'm going to grow a pony-tail too. *(to audience)* For weeks, the whole school discussed Ioane's pony-tail. No one knew the reason, though Veronica Crombie had a theory.

VERONICA: It's simple, he wants to be a girl.

PETER: Stephanie Arlington agreed.

STEPHANIE: You might be right Veronica, because Islanders wear dresses around the house.

PETER: Andrea Tudor had the real answer.

ANDREA: It's really hot in the islands, right, so they grow their hair really long, 'cos it's like an umbrella.

PETER: But Lorraine Carroll's theory was the most readily accepted.

LORRAINE: Dummies. In the islands they're really poor, and they can't afford scissors.

PETER: Lorraine you spaz, they live in New Zealand now.

LORRAINE: And they still can't afford scissors 'cos they spend all their money at the TAB and on booze. So there.

The boys play a round of peanuckle.

PETER and IOANE: Peanuckle. Peanuckle-peanuckle-peanuckle-peanuckle.

Suddenly they stop as they notice someone entering their classroom.

PETER and IOANE: Good morning Miss Hagan.

PETER: Miss Hagan was the only teacher I ever had who gave me nightmares – I was certain she was the witch from *Hansel and Gretel*.

MISS H: Good morning class. I hope we've all remembered our hankies. What do we say?

IOANE and PETER: *(chanting)* Before I go to school, I must brush my hair.

Ioane and Peter mime brushing their hair.

IOANE and PETER: Clean my tooth.

Ioane and Peter mime brushing their teeth.

IOANE and PETER: And I mustn't forget my handkerchoof.

Peter brings out a handkerchief and waves it in the air. Ioane does not.

PETER: Ioane!

IOANE: What?

PETER: Wave your hanky.

IOANE: I don't have one.

PETER: But you're meant to.

IOANE: But I don't have a cold. Look, no snot!

Ioane displays his nostrils.

PETER: Doesn't matter. Just wave your hand in the air.

IOANE: But I don't have a hanky. She'll see.

PETER: Old witches can't see very well. Haven't you read *Hansel and Gretel*?

IOANE: Who?

MISS H: Ian Tafioka, what are you doing?

IOANE: It's *Ioane*, Miss Hagan.

MISS H: Ian, you know your Islander name's too hard to say. Anyway, Ian's a lovely name.

IOANE: Ogay, Miss Hagan.

PETER: Miss Hagan, my father says that if you're going to change Ioane's name into English, then it should be John. Ian's not even a correct transliteration.

IOANE: John, I like John. It's in the *Bible*.

MISS H: Peter, there is no such word as 'transliteration', it's 'translation'. And if Peter doesn't want a smack on the back of his legs, he'll keep quiet. Anyway, there's three Johns in this class already, we're not having another one. Ian, where's your handkerchief?

IOANE: I'm waving it, Miss Hagan.

MISS H: I can't see it. Show it to me.

IOANE: It's a pretend handkerchoof.

MISS H: And why are you doing that Ian?

IOANE: Because Peter told me old witches can't see very well, like in the *Hansel and Gretel*.

Peter winces.

MISS H: I think Ian and Peter need to come up to the front of the class. John 2 – pass me that ruler. Ian, tell your mother to buy you a handkerchoof … chief.

Ioane and Peter bend over and wait to be hit on the back of the legs with a ruler. They flinch.

IOANE and PETER: Ow!!!

Music

PETER: *(to audience)* The next day Ioane didn't pick me up before school. He wasn't even at school. But on my way home, I met him in our street. He was helping his uncle carry a fridge. His mother and his Aunty Salote, who had a large moustache and the biggest bosoms I'd ever seen, were carrying heavy suitcases in each hand.

IOANE: Hey Peter. We're moving into number 26.

PETER: But we're number 28.

IOANE: That's right. We're your new door-next neighbours, next door. This is my mother.

PETER: Hello Mrs Tafioka.

MRS T: Hello Peter.

PETER: Welcome to Huntingdon Street.

IOANE: And this is my father.

PETER: Ioane's father was a big strong man. He wore a lavalava and jandals with white socks, and carried an entire couch under one arm. Mr Tafioka hardly spoke a word of English – he just beamed at me.

Mr Tafioka silently acknowledges Peter.

PETER: Ioane, where's the removal truck?

IOANE: Too expensive.

MRS T: Soso mai i

PETER: *(to audience)* No truck, not even a car, just the whole Tafioka family carrying food, furniture, a guitar and all sorts of other junk down our street.

MRS T: Hey Peter, you in Ioane's class at school eh?

PETER: Yes, Mrs Tafioka.

MRS T: You make sure he work hard. No mucking around.

PETER: I promise.

MRS T: That's my boy.

She smiles and hugs him, and lets out a high-pitched laugh, then.

MRS T: *(angrily, to her daughter)* Sulu, pick that up.

PETER: It was almost dark as my father drove home from university. *(to Dad)* Dad, this is Mrs Tafioka, Ioane's mum.

Dad smiles.

DAD: Gidday Mrs Tafioka – nice to meet you.

PETER: Mrs Tafioka was overjoyed, as Dad was the only adult in the whole street to welcome the new neighbours, and to learn their name. Meanwhile, on the other side of the road in the musty lounge of number 29, Mrs Heathcote opened the blinds to see what on earth was going on.

Mrs Heathcote opens the curtains.

MRS H: Bloody Islanders.

Music.

IOANE: Hi Miss Burton. My family would like to invite Peter to our house for lunch on Sunday.

MUM: How lovely. Tell your mother Peter would be delighted.

IOANE: Great. Tell him to be at our place at half past nine so we can go to church.

MUM: Church?

IOANE: We always go to church before Sunday lunch.

MUM: I'll make sure Peter's ready. Bye Ioane.

DAD: Ha, ha. My son the Christian eh?

PETER: You said I could go to Sunday School if I wanted.

DAD: Of course you can. Just don't expect me to have anything to do with it.

PETER: You drive me to clarinet lessons. Why not Sunday School?

DAD: Because religion is all rubbish Peter. It's made up. It's like the tooth fairy or Father…

MUM: Frank, don't you dare.

DAD: You can go to Sunday School, Scouts, Hitler Youth, or any other fascist organisation, as long as I don't have to hear them telling each other how bloody wonderful they are.

MUM: Church will be lovely Peter. They sing beautifully.

DAD: Oh, Jesus.

PETER: In their own language. I won't understand a word.

DAD: You wouldn't understand a word if it was in English, 'cos it's all bullshit.

PETER: Then how come I saw you reading the *Bible* at Uncle Max's funeral?

DAD: I was just checking that it was still all wrong, and it is.

PETER: So on Sunday morning, dressed in my best shorts, shirt, and an elastic tie, and enough Brylcream to kill every marine animal in the Pacific Ocean, I sauntered down to the Tafiokas. And as I reached their back yard, I noticed smoke. *(to Ioane)* Ioane, quick, your garden's on fire!

IOANE: Nah. It's our umu. That's where we cook our Sunday lunch.

PETER: You mean like a hangi?

IOANE: What's that?

PETER: It's what the Maoris do. They dig a hole in the ground, make a fire, put stones over it, then put the food on top and bury it.

Ioane laughs uproariously.

IOANE: Those silly Maoris. We put the stones on *top* of the ground.

PETER: Oh.

Mrs Tafioka proudly displays her garish hat to Peter, who is stunned by its tackiness.

MRS T: You like my hat Peter?

PETER: Oh yes. It makes you look so … beautiful, Mrs Tafioka.

MRS T: That's my boy.

Mrs Tafioka hugs him, pulling his face into her chest.

MRS T: *(angrily, to her daughter)* Sulu, stop that.

PETER: Hey Ioane, where's your church?

IOANE: Over in Newton.

PETER: But you guys don't have a car.

IOANE: That's why we catch the taxi.

PETER: So we crammed into the taxi – Mr and Mrs Tafioka, Ioane, his two older brothers, his little sister Sulu, and me. The driver didn't mind – he was Ioane's uncle. Outside the church were hundreds of Islanders, and Mrs Tafioka knew them all.

MRS T: Falu, this is my son Ioane, and this is my other son Peter. Ha, ha, ha. Can't you see the resemble? Ha, ha, ha. Sulu, stop that!

PETER: Inside the church, a large Island man appeared wearing a cheap suit.

CRIMINAL: Welcome to the house of our mighty God, our Father in heaven.

PETER: His trousers were too short, exposing a pair of white sports socks, each with different coloured rings, above his pointy vinyl boots.

PETER: Ioane, who in the hell's that?

IOANE: That's our minister.

PETER: Minister? He looks like a bloody criminal.

IOANE: A criminal? He does too, just like on the TV!

Ioane laughs.

PETER: Sshhh.

CRIMINAL: We also welcome our Palagi worshipper to our humble church. Let us sing our favourite hymn *Ia tia i ia le fefe.*

PETER: Hey Ioane, what does *Ia tia i ia le fefe* mean?

IOANE: My dick!

They both laugh. Ioane launches into the hymn.

IOANE: E le o le taumafai
E le o le usitai
Ui ina salamo ifo tagi ui o
E le faamagalo ai, ao 'oe le lavea'i
E le faamagalo ai, ao 'oe le lavea'i

Ua e togisala mai i lou maliu tiga
Ou te ofu atu nei ilau amio lelei
Ua ou sau ma lou nei mai
To lau pule e o la ai
To lau pule e o la ai

PETER: Mum was dead right about the singing. Once we got back, Mrs Tafioka disappeared into the kitchen while all the kids played on the front lawn. In half an hour the table was packed with food, but no one ate. The pork and chicken and taro sweated, and the chop suey congealed. The coconut bread and pagikeke begged to be eaten, but everyone just stood waiting. *(whispering)* Hey Ioane, when do we eat?

IOANE: You have to wait.

PETER: Why?

IOANE: You just do.

PETER: Then an orange Valiant Charger pulled up into the driveway. The back door opened and a huge man wearing reflective sunglasses surveyed the scene.

Criminal breathes heavily.

PETER: Criminal had arrived.

CRIMINAL: Lord. We are fankful to you that your church has profided this house for the Tafiokas. As we feast in this house, we fank God, we fank Lord Jesus, for looking after us all. Amen.

PETER: Now can we eat, Ioane?

IOANE: No!

PETER: Why not? He's said Grace.

IOANE: We have to wait for Criminal to eat first. It's a tradition.

PETER: Look. He's taking all the best food. Is that a tradition too?

IOANE: Nah, he's just a fat greedy pig.

They laugh

MRS T: Peter!

PETER: Yes Mrs Tafioka?

MRS T: You try this.

PETER: What is it?

MRS T: Raw fish. My special recipe.

Peter gags.

PETER: Raw fish? *(to audience)* The whole room stopped eating – even Criminal. Everyone looked at me – the only Palagi there.

Peter fearfully tries the raw fish. It's different, but okay.

MRS T: Do you like it?

PETER: Like it? I love it.

MRS T: See, I told you he was my son. Ha, ha, ha. Sulu, stop that.

Music. Dad surveys some bread on the table.

DAD: It took Western civilisation two thousand years to work out how to make leavened bread, but now every New Zealand housewife insists on baking these logs of gluggy, glutenous, toilet bowl-cracking brown bread.

MUM: It's coconut bread from Mrs Tafioka.

DAD: That's different.

He tries some.

MUM: Hypocrite.

DAD: This is bloody beautiful.

Mum tastes a bit.

MUM: Oh it is beautiful, Frank. We must do something for them. Mrs Tafioka always feeds Peter, and sends us parcels of food all the time. What do we do in return?

DAD: Bugger all.

MUM: Then why don't we invite them for dinner next Friday?

DAD: Of course. We've already got Graham and Bruce from the Drama department coming.

MUM: I forgot we'd invited them.

DAD: What do they do to homosexuals on the Tafioka's island? Stone them or put them in the stocks? Sure we'll invite the Tafiokas to dinner.

MUM: You make such a great show in front of your colleagues about living in a working class suburb, but you don't socialise with anyone from around here.

DAD: I know. Let's take Ioane and Peter to the beach next Saturday afternoon.

MUM: That's a great idea. *(pause)* Damn. We're going to the orchestra next Saturday.

DAD: Then the week after?

MUM: No. Ioane Tafioka is going to hear an orchestra too.

DAD: If you insist.

PETER: Next Saturday, we all got in the car and headed for the symphony orchestra.

DAD: No Marg, I'm not wasting money on a parking building. We'll find a park.

MUM: So Ioane, do your parents like New Zealand?

IOANE: Yes Miss Burton.

MUM: Your father works at the wharf, doesn't he?

IOANE: Yes, he's a seagull.

MUM: A what?

IOANE: He just works when they need him. He flies in one day, then flies away the next.

Ioane makes a seagull sound and laughs.

MUM: Does he like his job?

IOANE: Yes. 'Cos he's strong he earns lots of money. 75 dollars a week!

Mum tries to hide her surprise at the low amount.

MUM: That much?

IOANE: He says, 'in Niu Sila, every day is Christmas Day.'

MUM: So what does he actually do at the wharf?

IOANE: He unloads the ships, and at lunchtime he does the fishing. And the palagis say, 'what you doing Mr T, catching dinner? And he say 'yep'. Last night he brought home two gurnard, a terakihi and a barracuda.

MUM: In the harbour. That's extraordinary.

IOANE: And the terakihi was this big!

Ioane extends his hands.

IOANE: My island has the biggest fish in the whole world, Peter. One day you come home with me to the rock, Peter, and we catch the biggest fish together.

PETER: Yeah. One day. *(to audience)* Once Dad finally found a free park, we entered the hall.

IOANE: Hey Peter, you said the orchestra would sound good.

PETER: This is just the tuning up.

IOANE: My uncle tune his guitar when we do the hymns. Do you sing hymns at home Miss Burton?

MUM: No, we don't.

IOANE: I thought you liked music.

MUM: We love music, but we're not religious. Though I did sing in a church choir when I was young.

IOANE: How can you love music, but never sing?

MUM: Well I sing, but Peter's father doesn't like it 'cos he says I always get the words wrong. This piece is in four movements, Ioane, that means when the music stops, it's not the end, you don't clap.

IOANE: Why not?

MUM: You just don't.

IOANE: Okay. Even if I like it?

MUM: Even if you love it. You'll be able to clap really loudly after you hear a very fast loud bit – that's the presto, the final movement.

IOANE: *(whispering)* Peter, what's a presto.

PETER: My dick.

They both giggle.

PETER: Ioane really enjoyed the first movement.

The movement comes to an end. Ioane is just about to clap when Peter intervenes and puts his finger to his lips.

PETER: And he knew what to do at the end of the second movement.

The second movement ends. Ioane goes to clap but is just pretending. He gives the thumbs up to Peter.

PETER: But after the third movement an old lady behind us started to clap.

Ioane turns around.

IOANE: Shhhhh! Shaddup. You don't clap until after the pesto.

Ioane points to his head as if to say 'she' s crazy'. The symphony ends.Applause starts. Ioane grins. He won't clap. Peter starts to clap.

PETER: *(to Ioane)* It's okay, it's finished. You can clap.

Ioane takes the cue and starts to clap and cheer really loudly.

IOANE: Yay! Wo! Wo! Wo! Wo!

PETER: Then it was time for the soloist, a large soprano.

IOANE: Peter, that lady's really fat. And she's Palagi, too.

PETER: *(to audience)* After the violin introduction, the trumpets entered.

IOANE: *(whispering loudly)* Hey Peter, wouldn't it be funny if those violin sticks got stuck on the strings when they pulled them and they went like a bow and arrow – 'peoww, peoww'. It would hit the guys playing the trumpet right in the face!

Peter starts to laugh.

IOANE: Peoww, peoww!

PETER: Peoww, peoww!

PETER: As Ioane and I nearly wet our pants, Mum got the giggles as well. Dad just moved to the other end of the row, and pretended he didn't know us. The soprano also heard, and she was trying not to laugh while she sang. She succeeded brilliantly, and at the end of the piece we clapped and cheered.

IOANE: Yay. Yay. Pesto. Pesto. Thar she blows.

PETER: The conductor brought her out for an extra bow. She bowed low and, looking straight down at Ioane, gave him a massive wink.

IOANE: She winked at me, Peter. The fat lady winked at me!

Ioane winks back.

Music

In amongst the chirping birds, Mum and Dad sit on a rug at a picnic spot. Mum is gazing around; Dad is reading.

MUM: Oh Frank, this is the perfect spot for a picnic. We're so lucky the university own this place.

Dad grunts.

MUM: I think I can see a tui.

Dad sighs and continues reading.

DAD: *(without looking up)* Great, see if you can find another one.

MUM: I was just making conversation. Where are the boys?

DAD: Fishing.

MUM: They're not going to catch anything in that creek. It's tiny.

DAD: Course not, but Ioane found an eel gaffe in the shed. He was so excited, I let him try his luck.

MUM: I hope they were wearing sensible footwear.

DAD: Who cares? The half hour that kids spend exploring the wilderness is sacred …

An extremely excited Peter interrupts.

PETER: Dad, Dad! Look what Ioane caught.

DAD: Look at the size of it. Peter, get the knife.

MUM: Frank, we're not going to eat it.

DAD: Why not?

MUM: We don't have a licence. *(to Ioane)* Ioane, I think you should put the fish back in the stream.

DAD: Ioane, don't you bloody dare! *(to Mum)* We don't need a licence, stupid, 'cos it's not a trout. *(to Peter)* Peter, just stamp on its head.

MUM: Then what is it?

DAD: I dunno, but it's not a trout.

MUM: It's native, isn't it? Endangered probably.

DAD: No one's going to mind, we're miles from anywhere.

MUM: Isn't it you who always says that recreational fishermen are raping the rivers of this country.

DAD: It's different - Ioane's just a kid.

MUM: Really. Shall we tell that to the poor fish?

DAD: Don't be scared Peter. Stamp on it. Ioane, you stamp on it. It's bloody huge. Somebody stamp on it.

Mum stamps on the fish.

MUM: Alright. Just as well I brought some aluminium foil.

Ioane knocks on the Burton's door.

IOANE: Hello.

MUM: Hello Ioane.

IOANE: Is Peter around, Miss Burton? We were going to play the mini snooker.

MUM: I'm afraid his father's driving him to his clarinet lesson.

IOANE: Oh.

MUM: Ioane … where is Peter's mini-snooker set?

IOANE: At my place.

MUM: Then perhaps you could bring it back some time?

IOANE: Peter says he never play it here 'cos I get too excited and Mr Burton can't hear the Concert Programme.

MUM: You can borrow it any time you like, but it must live here. It's Peter's. He owns it.

IOANE: My brothers play with it too when Peter and I aren't using it.

MUM: That's fine, but at the end of the day, the mini-snooker set must come back here. It belongs to Peter. Do you understand?

IOANE: But Peter says he doesn't mind.

MUM: I don't care what Peter says. Can you go and get it now?

IOANE: *(ashamed)* No.

MUM: Why not?

IOANE: My uncles are coming tonight – for the tournament.

MUM: The tournament?

IOANE: Uncle Pou won 60 dollar last Friday. Maximum break of 147 twice in a row.

MUM: They gamble with Peter's mini-snooker set?

IOANE: It's okay, they pay him five dollars.

MUM: What did he do with it?

IOANE: Spent one dollar on lollies and lent the rest to Uncle Albie.

MUM: He lent money to your Uncle?

IOANE: He had to. Uncle Albie lose to Peter in poker.

MUM: What?!

IOANE: Full house to a straight flush.

MUM: Ioane, once tonight's tournament is over, I'd like you to bring Peter's mini-snooker set right back here. Understand?

IOANE: Yeah, I understand. Oh, another thing. My mother made you this basket to say fank you for taking me on the picnic all the time.

Ioane hands over a beautiful hand-weaved basket.

MUM: *(guilty as hell)* Oh it's … tell her it's absolutely beautiful.

IOANE: Ogay. See you.

PETER: The mini-snooker set was delivered back to its rightful owner. Just as well Ioane didn't tell Mum about my scooter – which had been living in the Tafioka's garage for over a year.

Mrs Heathcote approaches Mrs Burton.

MRS H: Pssst. They were having a party on Saturday night.

MUM: Morning Mrs Heathcote.

MRS H: I could hear the guitars and the singing.

MUM: The Tafiokas play guitars and sing every Saturday night.

MRS H: Those Islanders drink when they sing. And that's when they rape and murder.

MUM: Yes they were drinking on Saturday night. Cocoa – with lots of sugar. Peter had two whole cups with his pancakes.

MRS H: You let him go there?

MUM: Yes. But when I went to collect him there was no raping or murdering going on. Just a bit of praying, but that's okay in moderation.

MRS H: It's not healthy letting your boy play with those Islanders.

MUM: And how's your boy, must be forty soon?

MRS H: Next Saturday. We're planning a nice birthday dinner at home with his flatmates - nice boys - provided those Islanders don't make a noise. I'll call the police if they do.

MUM: Mrs Heathcote, the Tafiokas don't cause any harm.

MRS H: Yes they do. They use their stoves as heaters. You can always tell an Islander house 'cos the stove doesn't work properly. So there.

PETER: There was no party at the Tafioka's on Saturday night, so Mrs Heathcote could celebrate her son's birthday in peace. But there was a big event – an All Black test broadcast live from Wales.

DAD: So they all get up at some god-awful hour just to watch a stupid rugby game?

PETER: No Dad, they stay up and watch it.

DAD: Why do you want to watch rugby? It's a bloody awful sport.

PETER: It's live from Wales.

DAD: Can't work out why you like sport so much. Must be your mother's side.

MUM: Dad was a farmer, Frank. Everyone played rugby back then.

DAD: Tell me about it. I spent my whole childhood listening to people saying how bloody wonderful rugby was. All I wanted to do was play the piano but they'd all say 'why aren't you playing rugby, Frankie, your brothers are all playing rugby, Frankie, what's wrong with you, you girl.'

MUM: Well I think it sounds fun.

DAD: You despise the game, Margaret. You did everything you could to discourage Peter from playing.

MUM: Buying him a clarinet and a hockey stick is not discouraging him.

DAD: Let me tell you about the game of rugby, Peter. It typifies all the worst things about this country. It's violent, racist and elitist.

MUM: Come on Frank, you can hardly accuse the Tafiokas of being racist and elitist.

PETER: I noticed Mum left out violent. *(to Dad)* So can I watch the test at Ioane's, Dad?

DAD: Yeah, okay.

PETER: Thanks.

DAD: *(calling after)* Just don't expect me to be interested in the result.

MUM: Frank, why was Peter taking our spanner with him?

DAD: The switch on the Tafioka's stove is broken.

Music

PETER: All Ioane's relatives were there for the rugby, including Uncle Pou, who was always drunk.

UNCLE POU: You see the ruckby last week, Peter?

PETER: No, I didn't, Uncle Pou.

UNCLE POU: BG get three tries on the wing. But I'm the fastest winger in the country, and play for the best club in Niu Sila. Go the Ponsonby Ponies!

He makes a pony noise and hits the ground with his foot like a pony.

PETER: Since leaving the island, Uncle Pou had his moment of glory in his one game on the wing for the Ponsonby seniors when the great Bryan Williams was playing for Auckland and the other three Ponsonby wingers were injured. But Pou's rugby career came to an abrupt halt when he got into a scuffle in a bar. When the Auckland Police had finished with him, he was black and blue – the colours of his beloved Ponsonby club. Mrs Tafioka nursed her brother back to health until he was well enough to get into drunken brawls all over the city.

UNCLE POU: Ioane, give you friend some moneys so he can play poker with us.

PETER: Mrs T, how come all the bedding's in the TV room?

MRS T: 'Cos we all sleep there. It's the ruckby.

PETER: Everyone piled into the tiny lounge, where mattresses were laid down and blankets distributed. Mrs Tafioka brought in cocoa and we all tucked into Aunty Salote's freshly made pagikeke.

MRS T: Hey Peter. Your turn to sing.

PETER: But I don't know any songs, Mrs T.

MRS T: Then you do the nosewipe song again.

PETER: Please Mrs Tafioka.

MRS T: Peter. Do it! (singing) Peter, Peter, Peter…

Peter reluctantly assumes his position.

PETER: Before I go to school I must brush my hair, clean my tooth and I mustn't forget my handkerchoof.

He does the actions. Mrs T laughs and cheers.

MRS T: That's my son. So beautiful. Sulu, stop that!

PETER: Here come the All Blacks.

UNCLE POU: The All Black no good unless they pick me. 'Cos I'm the fastest winger in the country. Ha, ha, ha.

PETER: You faster than BG, Uncle Pou?

MRS T: My brother is much faster than BG, Peter, 'cos he practises running to the bloody pub every morning.

Mrs T cracks up then suddenly stops.

MRS T: Get up. National Anthem.

The boys stand (singing) 'God of Nations at thy feet'.

PETER: Next it was the Welsh turn to sing.

Peter/Ioane singing Bread of Heaven Bread of Heaven from 'Land of our Fathers'.

PETER: They barracked and sung like a bunch of Pacific Islanders. We cheered so loudly we would have woken up our entire street. But the entire street was already awake watching the game – except my parents who were fast asleep, probably dreaming of symphony orchestras. After the game, the Tafiokas talked more and more in their own language. I didn't understand what they were saying but it didn't matter. When television closed down, Mr Tafioka turned off the lights and we pulled up the blankets and drifted off to sleep – all of us together, snug and warm.

There is a loud, drunk snoring in the dark.

UNCLE POU: Eh what's happened?

PETER: All over Uncle Pou. We won.

UNCLE POU: I sleep through the whole bloody fing. Why no one wake me up? No one here like me?

He resumes snoring immediately.

PETER: Hey Dad, I've been put up to Standard One already.

DAD: That's great. What about Ioane?

PETER: He's still in the primers. Only some of us were put up.

DAD: Marg, I'm off to school.

PETER: I couldn't work out why Dad drove to school. The sun was shining. Even on the day of the *Wahine* disaster he'd said that school was close enough to walk to.

DAD: If you're going to promote Peter, Miss Hagan, then you should promote Ioane as well. They're exactly the same age.

MISS H: Mr Burton. It's not up to you to interfere in the education of another child. Besides, I think I know what's best. I've had a lot of experience with Maoris, Islanders, and other slow learners.

DAD: I'm well aware of your dealings with Polynesians, Miss Hagan. That's why I'm here.

MISS H: Not the strapping and smacking issue again is it? I have told you – they like it.

DAD: It is called corporal punishment, and it's illegal.

MISS H: Then I'll remind you it's also illegal to keep your child home from school without a good excuse.

She finds a note and reads it.

MISS H: 'Dear Miss Hagan. Please excuse Peter from school, he was doing his clarinet practice.'

She reads another note.

MISS H: 'Please excuse Peter from school, he was skiing with me.' And the best of all, 'please excuse Peter from school – I thought it better to keep him home.' What does that mean?

DAD: Peter is extremely unhappy that his best friend is no longer in the same class as he is.

MISS H: I'm afraid Ian's a bit slow.

DAD: His name is Ioane. At least get that right. And as a professional pedagogue, I have observed Ioane. He has made stunning progress in language acquisition and comprehension. And his genre recognition is outstanding.

MISS H: But Ian's maths is appalling.

DAD: Is that right? Then why can Ioane … divide fractions?

MISS H: I know he's very good at sport, and his art work's very … vibrant, but Ian Tafioka cannot divide fractions.

DAD: Would you like me to prove it?

MISS H: Mr Burton, if I promoted Ian, he'd hold other brighter children like Peter back.

DAD: Don't be so bloody stupid. Children of the same age who live in the same area should be in the same class. That is why education in this country is state, free, and secular for Christ's sake. You employ outmoded techniques like rote learning and corporal punishment. Furthermore, every single Polynesian child at this school is held back because you, Miss Hagan, believe they're inferior. I will take you to court if you do not put Ioane in the same class as Peter.

MISS H: Mr Burton, I do not appreciate being threatened with legal action or being called racist. And I'll have you know I have a lick of the tar brush myself. As for Ian Tafioka, he's staying right where he is. Goodbye Mr Burton.

DAD: Goodbye Miss Hagan.

PETER: Next morning, Ioane was put into my class, Sulu was put up to Primer Four, and Ioane's brothers were both put up a year. And his cousin, Salia, the only girl in Standard Two who had tits, was put way up to form two. Ioane had no trouble keeping up in maths – once Dad showed him how to divide fractions.

MRS T: Hello.

PETER: Hello Mrs Tafioka.

MRS T: Peter, Ioane is in your class now.

PETER: I know. Cool eh.

MRS T: Is your father here?

PETER: Sure. *(calling)* Dad! *(to audience)* When Dad came out, Mrs Tafioka just put her arms around him and gave him a great big hug. And he didn't even tell her to piss off like when Mum tried to hug him.

MRS T: We're having a party next Saturday night Miss Burton. Will your family come?

MUM: We'd love to. 8 o'clock at your place?

MRS T: 8 o'clock in the garage.

MUM: In the garage?

MRS T: That's right. My sister just get a job as a tea lady at the Department of Maoris Affair, and she's bringing some of them along. I don't want Maoris messing up my house.

PETER: The party was a success and the Maoris behaved themselves in the garage. Even Dad had a good time and danced. But Ioane and I had far more interesting things to do than go to parties.

Peter bowls a cricket ball – Ioane whacks it. Ioane's accent is now no longer fobby in any way.

IOANE: Six.

PETER: We played for hours in our differing styles. Ioane's favourite player was Gary Sobers.

Ioane whacks a four.

IOANE: Four.

PETER: While I preferred the more workmanlike Geoff Boycott.

Peter plays a forward defensive shot.

PETER: Ioane's sister, Sulu, liked to field.

Peter bowls a ball. Ioane whacks it. Sulu watches it drop to the ground and run past her.

PETER: Catch the ball, Sulu.

SULU: But I want a bat.

PETER: You don't get a bat unless you get your brother out. So concentrate. Now get the ball.

SULU: Shaddup. You get it.

PETER: You get it. I'm the bowler and you're the fielder.

SULU: But there's wetas in the bush. They might bite me.

PETER: There's no wetas in there. Go and get it or I'll put worms down your neck.

SULU: Oooo. I'll tell Mum.

Sulu carefully steps into the bush to field the ball.

PETER: Sulu watch out there's a giant weta! It's gonna bite ya.

SULU: Mummy!

Sulu runs away in terror while Peter laughs and laughs.

PETER: On Saturday afternoon Ioane and I would hang around Marewa Park just in case an adult team was short. *(to Indian man)* Excuse me, you guys need any players?

MR PATEL: Yes. Two of our chaps have to work in their shop today.

PETER: Overnight, Ioane and I became members of the Indian Sports Cricket Club.

MR PATEL: Okay chaps. That was a bloody good fielding effort. Here's our batting order: Patel D; Dulabh; Govind; Patel S; Patel M; Patel K; Patel K Jnr; Burrton – is that how you say it? Burr-ton.

PETER: Yep.

MR PATEL: And Tar… Tapioca

PETER: It's Tafioka.

MR PATEL: Okey dokey.

PETER: *(to audience)* Our opposition had a really fast bowler operating at one end, and a really clever spin bowler at the other.

MR PATEL: Bloody hell. 47–8. Get your eye in first, Burrton. And watch that fast bowler.

Peter blocks defensively.

MR PATEL: Well done, Burrton.

Peter blocks again. The ball hits him.

PETER: After ten overs I hadn't scored a run, but I was still there. And Mr Patel at the other end was scoring well until the umpire, Mr Patel Jnr, gave him out lbw.

MR PATEL JUNIOR: *(holding up his finger)* Sorry Dad, but you were jing-bang plumb in front.

PETER: Then Ioane came to the wicket.

IOANE: You take care of the fast bowler and leave me the spinner.

PETER: Okay.

Ioane hits balls all over the park.

PETER: Six. Four. Six. Four. Four. Four.

Peter blocks defensively.

PETER: Thanks to my defence and Ioane's attack, with one over to go we needed only five runs to win. Trouble was, I was facing and all I knew how to do was block.

Peter blocks.

PETER: *(he blocks)* No matter how I tried *(he takes a wild slash and misses)*, I couldn't penetrate the field *(he goes to drive but ends up blocking)*.

Ioane and Peter meet in the centre of the pitch, just like on television.

IOANE: Pssst.

PETER: What do you reckon?

IOANE: There's only one ball to come. You score a four, we only draw. You gotta hit a six.

PETER: I've never hit a six in my life.

IOANE: Then try.

PETER: *(to audience)* The fast bowler roared in. I could feel a six coming on. I lifted my bat up high — and got a thin edge. The gully fieldsman dived full-length and caught the ball in his fingers – then fell onto the ground and dropped it!

IOANE: Run Peter!!! Run.

They set off for the run in slow motion.

PETER: I sprinted for my end, Ioane for his. It was suicide. The slip fielder rushed in and fired the ball towards the bowler, who whipped the bails off straight away. I was way out of my ground.

MR PATEL JUNIOR: *(about to raise finger)* Oh bloody hell. That's it. Let's all go home.

PETER: But the bowler hadn't actually caught the ball. It had slipped through his fingers and was hurtling towards the boundary for four overthrows.

MR PATEL: Mr Burrton, you've gone and hit a bloody five!

PETER: Ioane and I brought glory to the Indian Sports 1D cricket team. Mr Patel K Senior insisted we pick any ice block we wanted from his dairy. Then he gave Ioane a great big bag of lollies for top-scoring with 88 runs. We walked home, arm in arm, extremely happy – until a familiar Holden Kingswood pulled up beside us. Funny how it only ever happened when I was with Ioane.

COP: Hello boys. Where have you been?

IOANE: Playing cricket, constable.

COP: Is that right? Who for?

IOANE: Indian Sports.

COP: Of course you would. Who's the captain of your team? Mr Patel is it?

IOANE: Yes.

COP: What a surprise. Own a fruit shop does he?

IOANE: No. Dairy.

COP: You think you're pretty smart, don't you? Where did you get those ice blocks?

IOANE: Mr Patel gave them to us.

COP: I see, you just walked into Mr Patel's dairy and he handed them over. Then he said, 'here, have some lollies too.'

IOANE: That's right.

COP: What's your name?

IOANE: Ioane Tafioka.

COP: What does your father do, Ioane?

IOANE: He's a seagull.

COP: Are you looking for a hiding?

IOANE: He works at the wharves.

COP: You boys are out late.

IOANE: Game went to the last over.

COP: Do your parents know you're out?

IOANE: No.

COP: *(into radio)* Two young shoplifters. One offender – Islander about fourteen.

IOANE: I'm ten, sir.

COP: Says he's ten. One Caucasian accomplice – same age. *(to Ioane)* And don't open those lollies.

IOANE: Sorry sir.

PETER: After checking with Mr Patel, the cops dropped us home. Ioane hadn't done anything wrong, but he still got a whack from his mother 'cos she didn't want him getting involved with the police. And while Ioane was a hit on the sports field, he wasn't doing as well as me in the classroom. Mum and Dad reckoned I should help him with schoolwork as much as I could.

DAD: Peter, where in the hell have you been?

PETER: At Ioane's.

DAD: But it's half past nine! You mother's been going crazy. She's out looking for you.

PETER: We were joining the library.

DAD: You already belong.

PETER: I was helping Ioane join.

DAD: That takes two seconds.

PETER: Not for Mrs Tafioka. She can't read. I had to wait for Mr Tafioka to come home.

DAD: And?

PETER: He was drunk.

DAD: Oh Jesus. You could have let us know.

PETER: I was only trying to help, but it's pretty hard joining someone up with the library when their father starts singing all the time and their mother can't write and we're trying to get a book and it's not my fault.

Peter bursts into tears.

DAD: I'm sorry. Did you join him up in the end?

PETER: Yeah. I filled the forms in myself and forged Mr and Mrs Tafioka's signature.

DAD: Well done. You're a good friend to Ioane, but don't tell your mother about the signatures. Was Mr Tafioka okay?

PETER: Yeah, but I have to see him first thing tomorrow morning.

DAD: What for?

PETER: He's going to pay me fifty cents to do his income tax.

Music

MRS T: Hello.

MUM: Hello Mrs Tafioka, how's the new job?

MRS T: It's a good job, Miss Burton. I'm tea lady at the Ministry of Foreigns Affair. But I got a big problem.

MUM: Is it money?

MRS T: No, put your purse away. Ioane's Uncle Teo is getting married to a Palagi.

MUM: That's nice.

MRS T: I dunno. I don't mind Palagis as neighbours, but I don't really want them as members of my family. Sulu!

As Mrs Tafioka goes to hit Sulu, Mum tries to stifle a laugh.

MRS T: What's so funny?

MUM: Oh nothing.

MRS T: But you're laughing.

MUM: I don't know how to explain.

MRS T: I thought English was your first language.

MUM: What you say about Palagis is exactly what many Palagis say about Pacific Islanders.

MRS T: You say that about us?

MUM: Oh no, I don't.

MRS T: Then what's so funny?

MUM: *(embarrassed)* Nothing. I'd be delighted to help. What would you like me to do?

MRS T: I need some help with the foods for the wedding. Palagi foods.

MUM: You just tell me what you want.

MRS T: Not much, just a wedding cake.

MUM: No problem.

MRS T: With the six layer and the white icing and the man and the woman on top.

MUM: I'd be delighted.

MRS T: And some sponge cakes.

MUM: Oh alright. How many?

MRS T: Forty. What's that Sulu?

Mrs Tafioka listens to Sulu.

MRS T: With the whipped cream and the strawberry jam. *(to Sulu)* Good girl for remember.

MUM: Of course.

MRS T: Thank you, Miss Burton.

PETER: So Mum, the feminist, put down her copy of *The Female Eunuch* and spent a week in the kitchen. The first wedding cake she ever made looked wonderful. It was only when the bride cut the cake that I realised she was a few months pregnant. *(to Ioane)* Hey Ioane, how come all your uncles only marry Palagi girls?

IOANE: Better looking.

PETER: What about your cousin, Malina? She's a spunk.

IOANE: You like her Peter. *(yelling)* Hey Malina, Peter loves you …

Peter restrains Ioane.

PETER: No, I just think she's a spunk.

IOANE: She's a spunk 'cos she's not married yet.

PETER: What's that got to do with it?

IOANE: You have to promise you will never share this secret I am about to bestow upon you.

PETER: Sure. What is it?

IOANE: *(confidentially)* This is knowledge that was passed down to me by Fakavakawaliwali, the witch doctor in our village.

PETER: Really?

IOANE: When Island women are young, they're very skinny and beautiful, just like Malina.

PETER: Yeah.

IOANE: So you get to know her, marry her, then sleep with her, though not always in that order. And on the night you're married, you're kissing in the dark and holding each other and when you touch around the top of her thigh you feel this piece of string. And as soon as they've married you, they reach for the piece of string and pull.

PETER: And what happens?

Ioane mimes a parachute expanding.

IOANE: Fwoooooossssshhhhh!!!!! She turns into a great big elephant. The piece of string is a parachute cord.

Ioane laughs and laughs.

PETER: Bullshit.

IOANE: You don't believe me. Aunty Leah, Aunty Llosa, Aunty Salote, Aunty Pua. All married, all skinny when they were young.

PETER: Aunty Foodtown Salote?

IOANE: Miss Pacific Princess, 1959.

PETER: You're being really racist.

IOANE: How can I be racist? I'm a boonga.

PETER: So you gonna get a Palagi girl pregnant and marry her?

IOANE: No way.

PETER: All your uncles have.

IOANE: I'll get a Palagi girl pregnant, then be like my cousin Uli and piss off to Australia.

Music. There is a knock on the door.

MRS T: Hello.

MUM: Morning Mrs Tafioka. How are you?

MRS T: I don't know where to send Ioane next year. Are you sending Peter to the boys' school Miss Burton?

MUM: No, Frank and I prefer co-educational schools.

MRS T: Our Minister says the boys' school is the best one in Wellington.

MUM: Well, Frank — Mr Burton — doesn't think so.

MRS T: Ioane won't do any work if there's girls around. He's like his brothers.

MUM: Frank thinks Prince of Wales High is very good. Excellent art and music.

MRS T: My sister clean at the Educations Department. Milk and three sugars please. She says Prince of Wales is shit. No uniform, do what you like all day, and if the kids give the mouth to the teachers they not allowed to give them a whack. And they have to learn the Maori too. What sort of job they gonna get with that?

MUM: Mrs Tafioka, I can't advise you where to send Ioane. It's up to you to choose what's best.

MRS T: If you send Peter to Princess of Wales, then that's good enough for me.

MUM: Good, but as I said, it's your choice.

MRS T: Okay. Do you have the Krispy biscuit with the coconut?

PETER: So Ioane and I both enrolled at Prince of Wales High, and we looked pretty cool in our uniforms.

IOANE: Hey Peter, what class you in?

PETER: 3F. And you?

IOANE: 3A. So who's the dummy?

PETER: They don't stream at Prince of Wales.

IOANE: Didn't you ask to be in my class?

PETER: Yeah, but they said there were lots of things they had to take into account. *(to audience)* Of course, Prince of Wales High did stream, it's just they called it banding. Ioane's class was called 3A after their boring form teacher Mr Anderson. My class was called 3F after Fiona, a drama teacher who didn't believe in last names. While the Islanders in 3A copied notes and got detentions, the Palagis in 3F visited art galleries and made films. But in the weekends Ioane and I still hung out together. And no matter where we went, our friends were never far away.

COP: Hello boys

PETER: Afternoon cont-stable.

COP: It's constable. What are you boys up to?

PETER: *(to audience)* Ioane didn't say a word, he just handed over a beautifully laminated sheet he'd made in Art the day before.

COP: *(reading)* 'Hello constable. My name is Ioane Tafioka, but if you really want to, you can call me John or Ian. I live at 26 Huntingdon Street. No, I'm not a Maori, I'm a Pacific Islander. No, I'm not an overstayer, I have a New Zealand passport. No, I do not know anything about recent burglaries in the area. Have a nice day.' *(to Ioane)* You think you're bloody clever don't you?

PETER: Ioane silently took his laminated sheet and we walked home laughing and laughing. But as the year went on, things started to change. At lunchtime Ioane would hang out, smoking, behind the basketball courts with his mates in the bottom class, while I would rehearse with the orchestra. We'd hardly see each other, until one week in the fifth form …

IOANE: You're playing what?

PETER: A cowboy in *Annie Get Your Gun*.

IOANE: Are you gay?

PETER: No. We get out of school for the whole last week of rehearsal. You should audition.

IOANE: I'm sure they need a brown cowboy.

PETER: No, they need a Big Chief Sitting Bull.

IOANE: I see. Hire a boonga to play the dark guy.

PETER: You got it.

IOANE: No way, I can't sing.

PETER: Big Chief Sitting Bull doesn't have to sing. He just stands there with his arms crossed and looks brown. Well … red, actually.

IOANE: Give me one good reason I should do it.

PETER: Lisa Pearson's dancing in the chorus.

IOANE: Lisa 'I like 'em dark' Pearson?

PETER: The white girl with the jungle fever.

Ioane crosses his arms red-Indian style.

IOANE: What do I have to do — um?

PETER: Nothing. I've already told Fiona you'd do it.

IOANE: You bastard.

PETER: Next rehearsal's on Monday at 8.

IOANE: p.m?

PETER: a.m.

IOANE: No way.

PETER: Don't be a lazy Islander, just do it.

IOANE: Okay.

PETER: Rehearsals were great fun, and Ioane turned up on time to every one.

IOANE: 'Sitting Bull live by three rule. Keep bow tight. Keep arrow sharp. No put money in show business.'

PETER: Mum worried that I was missing so much schoolwork, but Dad had no such worries.

DAD: It's bloody great. He's out of here by 7.00am, then we don't see him until after eight at night.

MUM: But it's his School Cert year, Frank.

DAD: He'll pass. The hours a teenage boy spends socialising with his peer group are sacred.

PETER: Fiona thought Ioane had real talent.

Ioane crosses his arms and speaks slowly and forcefully.

IOANE: Annie Oakley win match; lose Frank. Annie lose match; win Frank. We make peace medicine.

PETER: And Lisa Pearson always seemed to be doing leg stretches when Ioane was around.

Lisa bends over and stretches her legs, pointing her bottom right towards Ioane.

IOANE: Hi Lisa.

LISA: Hi Ioane. Nice moccasins.

IOANE: Thank you. Nice thong.

PETER: But on the day the show was to open, Fiona got a phone call from the police.

DAD: *(on phone)* You're where, Peter?

PETER: At the police station, Dad.

DAD: What have you done?

PETER: Nothing. It's Ioane. He got drunk at the pub at lunchtime.

DAD: What was he doing in a pub?

PETER: The half-hour a kid spends drinking beer at lunchtime is sacred …

DAD: Peter, this is no time for joking.

PETER: Can you come over and bail him out?

DAD: What about his parents?

PETER: Dad. Most parents work more than two hours a day.

DAD: I'll be there right away.

PETER: Thanks Dad. Don't forget your chequebook. *(to audience)* Dad bailed out Ioane then we dropped him off with Fiona in the school music room where Ioane chundered all over an autoharp. *(to Ioane)* Hey! You're on in five minutes.

IOANE: *(groggy)* I can't go on, man, I'm still pissed.

PETER: Just speak slowly and you'll be fine. *(to audience)* The school hall was packed, and the Tafiokas were all there in their Sunday best. Even Criminal turned up. The school orchestra finished the overture, then Ioane appeared.

Ioane takes a big breath, and walks onto stage. He crosses his arms red-Indian style. He is about to vomit, maybe he does a little bit, but just swallows again. He speaks very slowly and clearly.

IOANE: Big Chief Sitting Bull on way home from Washington. Go see Great White Father about Indian territory.

PETER: Ioane spoke just like an Indian Chief should. He was the hit of the show.

CRIMINAL: Ioane that was a wonderful, a wonderful …

MUM: Well done, Ioane. That was beautiful, Reverend Alisi.

CRIMINAL: A wonderful …

Criminal is distracted by Lisa.

LISA: Hey Ioane, you were so cool. The after-show party's at my place.

CRIMINAL: Wonderful …

LISA: Are you going to come?

CRIMINAL: … performance.

PETER: Then a big hand grabbed Ioane's shoulder. It belonged to Mr Tafioka. Mr Tafioka who hardly ever spoke, and this time he wasn't smiling.

MR T: Ioane has to be with his family tonight

PETER: Mr Tafioka, the opening night party's a sort of tradition …

MR T: No Peter. I said Ioane is coming home. Now!

PETER: We gave the Tafiokas a lift home. No one said a word the whole way. When we stopped outside their place, the Tafiokas led their condemned son into the house, while my parents just sat there. Dad, who'd courageously debated the issue of corporal punishment in schools live on TV with a National Party cabinet minister, suddenly didn't have the guts to tell his angry neighbour not to hit his son. And Mum, who'd spoken at nearly every playcentre in the country, telling mothers how to discipline their kids without hitting them, suddenly found it impossible to provide Mrs Tafioka with an alternative to beating the crap out of Ioane. We drove slowly up the driveway in guilty white silence.

Once inside, Mr Tafioka asked Ioane's brothers to lay into him with a stick, because his court appearance was going to bring the family so much shame. Then Mr Tafioka grabbed Ioane's school cricket trophy and whacked it over his head, bending it way out of shape. When Ioane didn't apologise loudly enough, Mr Tafioka got so angry he grabbed his machete and slashed it at his son, just missing him.

There is a quiet knock. Ioane has his head bowed. He is deeply ashamed

IOANE: Hello.

MUM: Morning, Ioane.

IOANE: Miss Burton. I've come to apologise for my behaviour yesterday. Peter, I am sorry for shaming you in front of your father, and our classmates. Miss Burton, I am sorry for disappointing you after all the help you've given me. Mr Burton, thank you for bailing me out. I promise you will get your money back.

MUM: Thank you Ioane, your apology is accepted.

COURT OFFICIAL: All rise for Judge Parsons.

JUDGE: Mr Ioane Vikelu Tarfuckiofa. Underage drinking in a bar is a very serious offence. Nevertheless, if that is all you had done, I would have been inclined to show leniency. However, drinking enough alcohol to reach such a state of intoxication that you still can't remember throwing a beer jug through the television screen of a public bar while you should have been in school cannot be tolerated. And the loss of the last eight New Zealand wickets for thirteen runs does not qualify as an excuse. As for entering a construction site — that was plainly stupid behaviour. How you managed to get into a crane and actually drive it thirty metres is beyond my comprehension. It is just as well your excessive intake of alcohol caused you to stall the crane, thereby avoiding a possible tragedy. Do you have anything to say in your defence?

IOANE: I'm very sorry.

JUDGE: Speak up boy!

IOANE: I'm very sorry and deeply regret my actions.

JUDGE: If it were not for the stunning character references provided by Reverend Alisi and Mr Burton, I would have no hesitation in imposing a custodial sentence. Mr Burton, I agree that the years spent experimenting in adolescence are formative and, as you say, sacred, but the boy must learn. Tarfuckiofa — I'm sentencing you to 50 hours of community service for the Pacfic Island Associated Church that the Reverend Alisi will supervise.

IOANE: Thank you sir.

PETER: Ioane helped do up the pool room in Criminal's house, then it was exam time. He didn't turn up to Maths and walked out of English after ten minutes. He'd been averaging 70s all year in Art, but got stoned before the exam and sat at a desk writing his name 2000 times. He left school, went on the dole, and hardly ever came home. I had problems of my own. I was captain of the cricket team, prizewinner in English, Maths and Maori, but couldn't find a date for the end-of-year social. As I was walking home one day, I saw this gorgeous babe in tight jeans, coming out of the Tafioka's house. Sulu?

SULU: Hi Peter. How's it going?

PETER: Fine. How's school?

SULU: A lot stricter than your one. Heaps of homework.

PETER: Your mum said you were working hard.

SULU: I passed all my exams this year.

PETER: Great. *(to audience)* You spend ten years teasing your best mate's little sister. Then she turns 15 and you suddenly realise she's a real spunk! Yet while you're trying to impress her, you can't help but remember when she was 5 years old, and you put worms down her neck to make her cry. Why did I do it? Why?

SULU: So are you guys having an end-of-year social?

PETER: Yeah, next Friday.

SULU: Mum's really strict about me going out since Ioane got into trouble.

PETER: Yeah. I understand.

SULU: But if she knew the guy …

PETER: Maybe you could go with me.

SULU: That'd be so cool.

PETER: Perhaps I could ask your mum.

SULU: No need, she says it's fine. See you Friday?

PETER: You bet.

Loud disco music. Sulu looks at Peter seductively for him to come over and dance. He is too shy. She walks over and grabs him. They dance. Peter is a truly terrible dancer.

PETER: At the social, Sulu looked like Donna Summer. We danced all night, and my mates from the cricket team were so jealous. They wanted to hear every detail of my budding romance.

TAMATI: Did you score?

PETER: Don't be disgusting.

TAMATI: You haven't even scored?

PETER: This is our first date. She's my best mate's sister.

TAMATI: Are you gay, Pete?

PETER: No I'm not.

TAMATI: Just questions man. Just questions. Can I have her after you?

PETER: Tamati! *(to audience)* After the social, I walked Sulu home, and we talked all the way.

SULU: You're such a good dancer.

PETER: Thanks, I've been practising.

SULU: Yeah, I can see that.

PETER: What time did your Mum say you had to be in?

SULU: She didn't. She trusts you.

PETER: Good. *(pause)* Well I suppose I should be getting going then.

SULU: I really enjoyed tonight, Peter. Thanks.

PETER: It was neat. You doing anything in the holidays?

SULU: Why? You planning to stick some worms down my neck?

Peter laughs, but is cringing on the inside.

PETER: I just thought we could go to the movies.

SULU: I'd like that.

PETER: Well. Goodnight.

SULU: Goodnight.

Sulu waits to be kissed by Peter. He kisses her. As he finishes kissing her he is very excited.

PETER: Yes!

IOANE: Get your hands off my sister.

PETER: Ioane. Haven't seen you for ages. What are you doing here?

IOANE: I live here. Didn't you hear me? I said get your hands off.

PETER: I was just saying goodnight.

IOANE: Didn't look like it to me. Sulu, get inside.

PETER: Come on man, what's with the protective brother crap.

IOANE: It's not crap, and keep away. Come anywhere near her again and I'll do ya.

PETER: What's up with you, man?

IOANE: Shaddup.

PETER: I see. It's fine for you to shag Lisa Pearson and every other white slapper at school, but I'm not allowed to kiss your sister goodnight. What's that all about? Let me talk to Sulu.

IOANE: I said stay away.

PETER: Come on Ioane, don't be stupid.

Peter pushes forward. Ioane pushes him back.

IOANE: Stay away.

IOANE: *(to Sulu)* Get inside, now!

PETER: *(to audience)* I stayed away. A couple of days later, Lisa Pearson found out she was pregnant, so Ioane followed cousin Uli and pissed off to Australia. When exam results came out, my cricket mates bought six bottles of Southern Comfort and we went off to a friend's bach for a drunken week to celebrate. When I got back, I noticed the Tafioka's house was empty.

NUN: Hello dear.

PETER: Who are you?

NUN: Sister Angela.

PETER: Where are the Tafiokas?

NUN: They moved out yesterday.

PETER: Why?

NUN: House has been sold.

PETER: But the church owns their house.

NUN: That's right. And they've sold it.

PETER: Bloody Criminal.

NUN: It's sad. But I wouldn't say it's criminal.

PETER: What is it — a block of flats?

NUN: No, dear, they're turning this house into a community centre. I run the meals-on-wheels. It's got a wonderful big kitchen with an excellent gas oven.

PETER: Yeah – makes great pagikeke.

NUN: Really. What's pagikeke?

PETER: My dick *(to audience)* I was certain Criminal was behind the eviction, but he had nothing to do with it. The new bishop from England didn't think it was the church's job to provide cheap accommodation any more. Mr Tafioka retired from the wharf, and Mrs Tafioka was replaced at the Ministry of 'Foreign Affair' by a cafe bar. The only place they could afford to rent was out in Mangere. The new community centre was a big hit and the whole street got involved — except Mum. She'd say 'why have a community centre when you destroy the centre of the community to build it?'

Hip-hop music.

PETER: A week after I'd run into Ioane at the TAB, I found myself outside it again. I had to go back in.

Peter walks in. Ioane sees him and sighs. Ioane's annoyed and ignores Peter.

PETER: Hey Ioane.

IOANE: Melbourne Cup's not for another year.

PETER: I'm not here to bet. Just wanted to catch up with an old mate.

Ioane ignores Peter for a while, then moves towards him. Peter thinks Ioane is coming to talk to him, but he's simply placing another bet. Ioane walks to the window.

IOANE: Five dollars each way on *Jonah's Wife*.

Ioane gets the bet then resumes looking at the screen.

PETER: Thought you said it was a donkey?

Ioane completely ignores Peter.

PETER: Hey, I just wanna talk.

IOANE: I'm busy.

PETER: I'll wait.

More silence. Ioane waits but Peter doesn't leave.

PETER: You good?

Irritated, Ioane turns around.

IOANE: Oh yeah, I'm great. I've got five kids to three different mothers, I've got four government departments chasing me for money I don't have. I'm up to my eyeballs in debt and I'm a certifiable alcoholic. It's the only certificate I've ever won.

PETER: And now you're living on the island. Great.

IOANE: It's a real Pacific paradise. The best place in the world to avoid paying maintenance to those Aussie bitches. So yes, Peter, life is fantastic. Happy?

PETER: Very happy. If you've gone back to your roots.

IOANE: Jesus you Palagis love that roots crap. They should have shot Bob Marley, not the sheriff. You're all the same: you find a brown kid next door and you think you can save him by signing him up to the local library.

PETER: Bullshit.

IOANE: I never even wanted to join that useless library! And now you save little brown kids for a living and get paid heaps for it. How lovely and bicultural. Congratulations Peter, you are richer for having known me. Much richer.

PETER: I am richer.

IOANE: Bullshit. Now if you'll excuse me, my race is about to start.

PETER: Then let me help you. What do you normally bet? Two dollars each way? *(to attendant)* Twenty bucks. No, fifty bucks on number 7. Give the ticket to this loser.

IOANE: Shut up.

PETER: Don't worry, I'm putting it on for my poor mate who's had such a terrible life. Number 3, *Ebony and Ivory*. How appropriate. 100 bucks.

Peter slaps down money.

PETER: Go on. Let's waste it all.

Ioane drags him to the other side away from his friends.

IOANE: Just get out and leave me alone.

PETER: Oh. Poor old Ioane. All these terrible people make him drink and gamble, even when he doesn't want to.

IOANE: I said shut up.

PETER: They hold him down, force his mouth open and pour beer down his throat, and then all these Aussie bitches sit on his dick and won't let him use a condom. Poor Ioane.

IOANE: Shut up. *(to other guys at the TAB)* What are you laughing at?

PETER: Isn't it interesting how nothing in your entire sad life has ever been your fault?

Ioane goes to hit Peter.

PETER: What are you going to do? Hit me? Go on.

Ioane backs off — humiliated.

PETER: Sometimes I see your mother waiting at the bus stop. I think I should stop and give her a lift and catch up, but then I wonder what the hell I can say. If I mention you she'll just say 'that shit'. So I just drive on by and pretend I didn't see her. But I thought it might be different with you. I thought we just might try and keep in touch. I don't want to reform you, or even help you. I just wish we could be friends. But don't worry mate, next time, I'll just walk on past and pretend I never ever knew Ioane Tafioka.

Peter goes to leave.

IOANE: That's not my name anymore.

PETER: Then what is?

IOANE: On the island they call me Kapisinga.

PETER: What does Kapisinga mean?

IOANE: My dick.

They both laugh.

IOANE: I don't hate you Peter. But I am going back to the island tomorrow.

PETER: I believe you.

IOANE: Maybe next time we could get together.

PETER: That'd be great. I'd love you to meet my partner Joss.

IOANE: Finally scored, eh Peter?

PETER: Finally.

IOANE: Nice guy this Josh?

PETER: She's Joss. And our son's Jack.

IOANE: A boy. That's great. And you're still living with the mother?

PETER: Yeah.

IOANE: Tell you what, why don't you come and visit me on the island. You and Josh and Osh-Kosh.

PETER: Why not? We might just do that.

IOANE: I'd love to show you all the interesting things on my island. It'll take about half an hour.

PETER: Then we'll go fishing eh? On the rock?

IOANE: Yeah. On the rock.

PETER: I better get going.

IOANE: Hey Peter.

PETER: Yeah?

IOANE: Say hi to your parents for me.

PETER: Of course.

Before Peter goes, he and Ioane hug. Ioane looks around.

IOANE: *(to TAB guys)* Shut up. We're not gay. Watch the races.

PETER: I planned the trip to the island — and even got a postcard from Ioane recommending a good place to stay. Then just before we were about to leave, I got a letter from a woman I didn't even know. Ioane had been stone-cold sober for over six months, and was living with a local girl — he'd finally succumbed to the parachute cord. Ioane got up one beautiful sunny morning. And as he did every morning, Ioane went out onto the big rock and fished.

IOANE: *(as a child)* My island has the biggest fish in the whole world, Peter. One day you come with me to the rock, Peter, and we catch the biggest fish together.

PETER: And he caught some fish. Big fish. Then it came, crashing over the rock. It wasn't alcohol, gambling, or even a hijacked crane that killed Ioane. It was a big wave on a small rock on a tiny island in the middle of a gigantic blue sea.

I don't go back home much now, except to visit my parents. Joss and Jack and I live in a town house in the trendy part of the city, and there are no Islanders around. The only tapa cloth in the street is at the local cafe — which does a lovely flat white. In fact, the whole neighbourhood's flat and white ... almost.

There is a knock on the door.

PETER: Hello?

A Chinese boy enters.

BOY: Hi. Where Jack?

PETER: He's in his room.

BOY: Good. He say he show me his new PlayStation.

PETER: Did he? Then I better call him. *(calling)* Jack! Someone to see you. *(to boy)* What's your name?

BOY: Wincen.

PETER: I'm Jack's father — Mr Burton. Nice to meet you Win Cen.

BOY: No, stupid. Wincent.

PETER: Oh. Vincent.

BOY: That's what I say. You deaf?

PETER: And where are you from, Vincent?

BOY: Next door. We just move in.

PETER: I meant what country do you come from?
BOY: Why you not say so, silly? I come from Hong Kong.

PETER: It's very nice to meet you, Vincent. *(calling out)* Jack, you've got a visitor. *(to Vincent)* Come on through. *(to Jack)* Hurry up!

Peter and Vincent exit.

THE END

ENGLISH ACTIVITIES
Knowing your way around the text

Activity 1

Find a quotation from the play that supports the statements below. Work through the play chronologically. Copy each statement and follow it up with your chosen quote.

- There has been some sort of conflict between Peter and Ioane at the beginning of the text.
- Peter and Ioane had last seen each other some time ago.
- Peter's upbringing has been different from Ioane's.
- Children learn their opinions from their parents.
- Ioane's teacher is racist.
- Mr Burton is unlike the other people who live on Huntingdon St.
- Ioane mispronounces English words.
- Peter becomes more comfortable at Ioane's home than his own.
- Mrs Tafioka has her own issues with race.
- The police react stereotypically to Pacific Islanders.
- Mrs Burton is genuinely happy to help Mrs Tafioka.
- The school treats students differently according to race.
- Peter and Ioane begin to take different paths.
- Differences in the discipline used between the Burtons and the Tafiokas.
- Romance blossoms between Sulu and Peter.
- Ioane puts a stop to the romance between Sulu and Peter.
- Peter thinks Ioane is a hypocrite.
- Ioane leaves New Zealand.
- The reason why the Tafiokas had to move.
- Mrs Burton's opinion of the new community centre.
- Peter really wants to see Ioane again.
- Ioane's opinion of Peter's job.
- What adult Peter thinks of Ioane's decisions.
- Ioane and Peter begin to sort out their differences.
- Ioane dies.
- Adult Peter thinks the neighbourhood he lives in is lacking personality.

Activity 2

There are several links between the beginning and end of the play. Before you begin the following tasks we suggest you send time reading pages 10-13 and pages 63-68.

Adult Peter and Ioane

The play opens with Peter and Ioane in the TAB. There is an obvious history between the two men and having read the play you will know that, towards the end, the relationship between Peter and Ioane is beginning to break down. The play ends by coming full circle and having the men back in the TAB.

1. Explain why you think this is an effective way to begin and end the play. Why not have just told the story chronologically from beginning to end?
2. Peter tries hard to be positive in both these scenes while Ioane is obviously quite happy to hold a grudge. Find several quotations that show each of the character's reactions to other.
3. Explain what Peter means when he says to Ioane: 'Isn't it interesting how nothing in your entire sad life has ever been your fault?'
4. How do you know that Peter and Ioane are likely to sort out their differences?

Young Peter and Ioane; Jack and new neighbour

At the beginning we meet a young Peter and Ioane. At the end of the play there is a similar scene between Peter's son Jack and his new Asian neighbour.

1. Using detail from the play, describe the connection between these two parts of the text.
2. Why do you think the playwrights decided to end the play like this?
3. What do these scenes say about New Zealand society?

Ioane's return to the islands

Early in the play Ioane tells Peter: 'My island has the biggest fish in the whole world, Peter. One day you come home with me to the rock, Peter, and we catch the biggest fish together.' (page 29). At the end of the play Ioane is back in his homeland and dies while fishing.

1. Select and write down significant quotations from page 10-13 and page 63-68 that outline the full circle of the Peter and Ioane's relationship.

Link to NCEA:

Use the information you have gathered above to help you answer the essay question below. You might find it useful to do some work on theme (pages 73-75) before you do so.

Describe an important scene at (or near) the end of the text.
Explain how this scene helped you understand an idea (or ideas) in the text.

Tip: *Although the essay does ask you to describe a scene this should not be the main focus of your essay. The second part of the question is where the marker will expect you to 'respond' to the text – to make connections and links between the scene you have described previously and your chosen theme. Therefore the majority of your essay needs to explain carefully how the scene helped you understand an idea.*

There are several scenes you might choose in order to respond to this topic but, for the purpose of this activity, we suggest you use pages 67-68 . This scene allows you to talk about the fact that history is repeating itself and that hopefully things will be different in the New Zealand Jack grows up in. You could use the information on Stereotyping (page 74) to help you.

Activity 3

Write a review of the play as a written text. Sometimes the hardest thing is to decide what it is about your text that makes it unique and interesting. Look at the questions below to help you formulate the content of your review.

Plot

Are you hooked right from the start?

Can you feel the atmosphere the author is trying to create?

Could you put yourself in the story?

Is the plot plausible and easy to follow?

Does it keep you interested all the way through?

Does the story build to a climax?

Is there a satisfying ending?

Is it hard to put the play down?

Characters

Are the characters credible?

Can you picture them in your mind?

Do they have a real personality?

Do you care about what happens to them in the end?

Is the dialogue realistic/natural/appropriate to the character?

Do the characters develop throughout the story?

Purpose

Is the purpose of the story merely to entertain you or is the author trying to convey a message between/beyond the lines of the story?
What did you learn by reading this story?
What is/are the major theme(s) raised?

Setting

What is the setting and does it play a significant role in the work?

Language

Is the language appropriate for the audience?

Personal Opinion

Would it be one that you would like to keep for your children to read? Why?

Would you recommend it to other students of your age? Why?

Out of 5, how many stars would you give this play?

Activity 4

Before you move onto the formal study of this text we would like you to stop and think about the play and the ideas it raises.

1. Does the play leave you with issues you want discussed or questions you would like answered?

2. If you could talk to the author, what opinions/thoughts would you offer about the issues raised in the Niu Sila?

You may like to be brave and actually send your thoughts to one of the playwrights, in the form of a letter or email. Send your letters or emails to Playmarket and they will forward these on to Oscar and Dave. The address for Playmarket is on page 88.

Theme

'Even though it's full of crack-up comedy,' says co-writer Armstrong, 'I look at *Niu Sila* as a sad play. 'It's a sort of a requiem to a time in New Zealand where white and brown kids grew up side by side. They went to the same school and their Dads and Mums often had similar jobs. Now that's all changed.'

Kightley, a Samoan, and Armstrong, a Palagi, had close childhood friendships with children from the 'other' culture. During the writing process they swapped their often hilarious stories of encountering each other's culture. 'I had some Palagi friends who I would visit for dinner,' remembers Kightley. 'All I wanted to do was silently eat their wonderful food, then perhaps talk afterwards, but the parents kept interrupting my eating with their polite dinner-time conversation. Their friendly questions, which I felt obliged to answer, kept stopping me from eating!'

Armstrong remembers the warmth of the communal style of living of his Pacific friends. 'My family was a comfortable and middle class nuclear one – Mum, Dad and four kids. Yet down the road my Pacific friends had aunties, cousins, and all sorts of people dropping in all the time. I remember envying my Pacific friends, even though they didn't have much money, and thinking their life was far more exciting than my boring middle class one!'

While much of *Niu Sila* relies on humorous childhood memories, there is also a serious undercurrent to the comedy and the play confronts issues such as violence and racism – both personal and institutional. 'I was never in trouble with the police as a kid,' explains Armstrong, who grew up in Wellington in the 1970s, 'but the minute I walked down the street with a Pacific Island kid, we would get stopped by the cops. We'd never done anything wrong, but they'd still stop us. That never happened when I was with Palagi friends'. Kightley got so sick of being stopped by police for no apparent reason that he made a laminated sheet humorously relating all his personal details. 'Every time I got stopped I'd just hand over the sheet,' says Kightley. This and other real-life incidents are used to humorous effect in the play.

As well as the politics of bicultural friendship, the sadness that often occurs as childhood friends grow up is also documented in *Niu Sila*. 'Outrageous comedy occurs when kids from different cultures grow up side by side,' says co-writer Dave Armstrong, 'and *Niu Sila* reflects this. But the play also chronicles the tragedy of cultures on a collision course. Kids grow up and suddenly close childhood friendships don't mean so much any more.'

Niu Sila sees it through white eyes, from Peter's perspective. It's more a play about the bicultural experience of immigration. It shows that Pacific migration has affected New Zealanders in more ways than just the clichés of sport and music. 'It's easier to be friends with someone when you are a kid — how good you are at backyard cricket or whether you get picked for the bullrush team is more important than where you come from.'

But kids grow up and cultures collide. It is the script's poignancy and thought-provoking portrait of a friendship caught in a cultural firing line that has Kightley bemused by the play being pitched to the public as an uproarious comedy.

Waikato Times Review 04 July 06

Part One: Stereotyping

An issue that arises from the play is that of stereotyping. Stereotyping is where people have an image of what a race or group of people is like and are unwilling to see them as individuals. Stereotyping is thought to drive prejudice because it involves generalisations.

1. Several characters in the play stereotype others. Look carefully at the table below and find TWO quotations from the play that support each character's viewpoint.

Character	Stereotypical viewpoint	Quotation 1	Quotation 2
Peter and Ioane's young classmates	Their opinion of Pacific Islanders.		
Mrs Heathcote (the neighbour)	Her opinion of her Pacific Islander neighbours.		
The Police	Their opinion of Pacific Islanders.		
Miss Hagan (school teacher)	The assumptions she makes about Pacific Island students.		
The School	The subjects taught to the Pacific Islanders vs. the Palagi.		
Ioane Tafioka	Lives up to the expectations put on him by others rather than fighting them.		

2. It is not only the Palagi characters in this text that have stereotypical views. Many of the Pacific Island characters have just as narrow a viewpoint of other people. In particular Mrs Tafioka. Find at least FOUR quotations from throughout the play that show Mrs Tafioka's view of both Maori and Palagi.

3. But (thankfully) other characters challenge stereotypes.
   Find TWO quotations for each character that give evidence that Peter and Mr Burton challenge the stereotypical views of their society.

4. Are there any other characters not mentioned previously that you feel either exhibit or challenge stereotypes. Explain, giving detail from the play.

Part Two: Acceptance of other people's culture

The next step in challenging stereotypes is to learn to accept other people and their culture/s. The writers of *Niu Sila* want to encourage New Zealanders to celebrate the Polynesian dimensions of the country we live in.

" 'I hope Palagi audience members who enjoy this play,' says co-writer Dave Armstrong, 'will entertain the idea that Pacific Islanders contribute far more to our society than cleaning our offices, singing beautifully, and scoring the odd try on the wing.' "

1. How do you think the play *Niu Sila* does this? Give reasons and details from the text to support your answer.

Other Themes you could look at:

- Friendship
- Being responsible for your own actions
- Pacific Island migration
- Violence.

Link to NCEA:

Use the notes you have gathered above to answer ONE of the essay questions below.

1. Describe an **important idea** you learned about in the text. Explain **why** this idea was **worth** learning about.

   Tip: *This essay is rather general but don't get trapped into thinking it is easy! It is obvious (hopefully!) that the first thing you need to do is describe one of the ideas you have looked at during your study of the play. However, many students may find the second part of the topic more difficult. The words in bold should help you. The question requires you to explain what is beneficial about students studying the text. Stop and think: why is it important for students of your age to read texts that are:*
   (a) about the country/community they are living in?
   (b) highlight both good and bad aspects of an idea/character/opinion?
   (c) demonstrate strong role-models?
   These ideas are a starting point only — think about other reasons it was worthwhile for you and your peers to read this play.

2. Describe a **surprising event** or **moment** in the text.
   Explain **how** this event or moment **helped you understand an idea (or ideas)** in the text.

   Tip: *Again this question asks for you to talk about an idea from the play but this time it is to connect it to an event or moment that illustrates the idea and therefore helps you to understand the idea. Choose your event/moment carefully. If you don't select an event or moment with enough material to talk about, your essay will be short and lack depth.*

Character

Forming character studies

Characters are very important in literary text. It is through them that we learn. Use the following questions to form character notes for Peter Burton and Ioane Tafioka.

- What do they look like?
  (Gender, age, hair colour, dress, clothing, distinguishing features etc)
- What is their personality like?
  (Cheerful, envious, sad, lonely, resourceful, scared etc)
- How do they speak?
  (How they say things can be a key to who they are. ie. colloquial = easygoing, aggressive = problem)
- How do they behave?
  (People are always judged by their actions)
- What problems do they encounter? How do they deal with them?
  (With people/themselves/environment) (Well? Why/ Why not?)
- How do they interact and act towards other characters?
  (Who do they feel comfortable with? If they are aggressive, why?)
- Do they change in any way? Why?
  (Appearance/actions/attitudes?)
  (What happened to bring about the change? An event? Action from someone else? Realisation?)
- How does this character help develop the issues and themes of the text?
- How is this character a role model for us?
  (What can we learn from them/their actions/ attitudes etc)

Link to NCEA:

Use the notes you have gathered above to answer ONE of the essay questions below.

1. Describe a **person** or **character** you **admired OR disliked** in the text.
   Explain **how** this person or character **helped you understand an idea (or ideas)** in the text.

   Tip: *Before you begin your essay it is important to think carefully about the words 'admired' (to have a high opinion of) and 'disliked' (to have an aversion to, to disapprove of). Think of each of the characters in the play – which falls into which category? Evaluate which character is going to give you the most scope for describing and explaining. It may not be the one you initially think about. Don't forget that your character needs to help you understand an idea in the text. You will need to make clear links between the two.*

2. Describe a **major change** in a **character or individual** in the text. Explain why this change was **important**.

   Tip: *The essay asks you to talk about change. The obvious character (but not necessarily the only character) to use for this essay is Ioane. The adult Ioane is a very different person from the young, carefree boy we first met. Look carefully through the notes you have created for Ioane to see what can be used in the essay. Don't forget that you will need to describe him both at the beginning and end of the text in order to show the change. Mentioning why the change occurred will also be expected. You will also need to explain the consequences and effects of this change.*

Character relationships

The chart below details the development of Peter and Ioane's relationship. Read it carefully.

Time of Life	Peter Burton	Ioane Tafioka
When we first meet Peter and Ioane they are adults of approximately 30. Obviously some history between them.	Tries to reignite friendship. Eventually gives up.	One word answers to questions. Aggressive, angry, thinks the worst in everything Peter says, for example, shouting him a beer.
Childhood: (from 5 years old)	New friend because of the cricket team.	Carefree ...happy … unconcerned with protocols (ie. not knocking, arranging things etc). Helps himself to food. Nothing puts him off his stride. Reservation – playing cowboys/Indians etc.
	Peter swears at his mother. (page 15)	Horrified at Peter's behaviour towards his mother. Makes him apologise.
	They don't believe in hitting. (page 15)	*... you'll get a whack* (page 15)
	I think we should finish chewing first. Mum says they should put soft padding underneath. (page 18)	*Let's play on the jungle gym.* (page 18)
	Peter is put into Standard One. (page 39)	Ioane is kept in the primers. (page 39)
Adolescents: (from 12 years old)	Genuinely part of the Tafioka family. (page 47/48) *... until a familiar Holden Kingswood pulled up beside us. Funny how it only ever happened when I was with Ioane.* (page 45)	
Prince of Wales High. First time the boys are not in each other's classes. Still walked to school with each other every morning.	3F (Palagis) visited art galleries, made films. (page 53)	3A (Islanders) copied notes, got detentions. (page 53)
But as the year went on things started to change. (page 53) Now only see each other on weekends. (page 53)	Peter would rehearse with the orchestra	Ioane would hang out, smoking, behind the basketball courts with mates in the bottom class. Underage drinking and bad behaviour lead to an arrest. Using drugs.
Now 16 years old and they hardly see each other. (page 58)	Captain of cricket team, prize winner in Maori, English, Maths.	When it came to School Certificate Ioane didn't turn up to the exams. Left school, went onto the dole, hardly came home.

Time of Life	Peter Burton	Ioane Tafioka
A 'budding romance' begins to take shape between Sulu and Peter.	*You spend ten years teasing your best mate's little sister. Then she turns 15 and you suddenly realise she's a spunk.* (page 59)	*Get your hands off my sister.* (page 61) Ioane goes to Australia to escape Lisa Pearson's pregnancy.
Play goes full circle and we are back to the present. Peter and Ioane (adults) are in the TAB.	Has a wife and son. *I don't want to reform you … I just wish we could be friends.* (page 65) *Then we'll go fishing eh? On the rock?* (page 66) Peter feels his neighbourhood is flat and white. (page 67)	5 kids to 3 different mothers. Four government departments chasing him for money. Alcoholic. *… you find a brown kid next door and you think you can save him by signing him up to the local library.* (page 64) *Maybe next time we could get together.* (page 65) *Tell you what, why don't you come and visit me on the island.* (page 66) Ioane dies while fishing.

Link to NCEA:

Use the notes you have gathered above to answer ONE of the essay questions below.

1. Show how EITHER **relationships** OR **conflicts** were important (or not important) in your studied text.

   Tip: *This essay gives you the choice of talking about the relationships or the conflicts in* Niu Sila. *The major relationship would be Peter and Ioane and the boys with their parents. You may also want to include some of the minor relationships: Sulu and the boys, the neighbours and Tafioka family etc. Whichever ones you decide to use you must explain why they are important … did they move the action?, show theme/s?, give us insight into a character?, did one character change how another thought or acted? etc. If you choose to talk about conflicts you need to think about internal and external conflicts and the effects of these. Conflict forms the heart of most dramas so take the time to think beyond the obvious.*

2. Describe **a main conflict** in a text you have studied **AND** analyse how the conflict helped the author to present important ideas.

   Tip: *This essay question works well for* Niu Sila. *The main conflict would have to be between Peter and Ioane and the question then asks you to explain how this conflict helped to show/ illustrate some of the important ideas in the play. You will need to look carefully at both your character and theme notes to effectively answer this question.*

3. Describe a **strong relationship** between at least TWO characters or individuals in the text. Explain **how** this relationship helped you **understand** these characters or individuals.

   Tip: *Again the question asks you to describe a strong relationship and again this relationship is most likely to be Peter and Ioane. The description of the relationship should come easily — particularly as it is outlined in the grid on the previous page! It will also be helpful to go back to the character notes you formed on the individual characters earlier in this section. The second part of the essay asks how the relationship helps you understand the characters themselves. Stop and think about what aspects of their personality are reflected in the relationship. Also think about what each character brings to the relationship and how the characters work together.*

Minor characters – Mr & Mrs Burton

Mrs Burton

- When she first meets Ioane she is very polite, despite the fact he just walked into her house unannounced!
- She happily converses with Ioane.
- Is happy for Peter to spend time with the Tafiokas. Wants to reciprocate by having Ioane spend time with them. (page 28)
- Struggles with some aspects of Pacific Island life ie. mini-snooker set going over to Ioane, but never stops it happening.
- Welcomes the Tafiokas into her home – makes Mrs Tafioka a cup of tea.
- Offers to give Mrs Tafioka money.
- Goes to a party in the Tafioka garage. (page 42)
- Defends the Tafiokas to the neighbours.
- Helps Mrs Tafioka with the wedding, ie. the makes the cake. (page 50)
- She works at 'talking to parents in playcentres 'telling mothers how to discipline their kids without hitting them'. (page 57) Hence she struggles with the violence in the Tafioka house (page 57) but says nothing.

Mr Burton

- Works at the university.
- A liberal.
- Only adult in the whole street to welcome the new neighbours, and to learn their name.
- Makes such a great show in front of colleagues about living in a working class suburb …
- Lets the boys be boys.
- Goes into bat for Ioane re. class placement. (page 40) He has previously done so about the strapping/corporal punishment of Pacific Island children.
- Bails Ioane out of the police station.

1. Create a similar character study to those above for the Burton's neighbour Mrs Heathcote.
2. Compare and contrast Mrs Heathcote and the Burtons. page 35
3. Describe the influence TWO minor characters had on each of the main characters.

Setting

My Auckland — by Dave Armstrong

Even though *Niu Sila*, the play I co-wrote with Oscar Kightley, is set in the heart of 1970s Ponsonby, I must confess that I am a Wellingtonian and at best only an honorary JAFA. That said, a large proportion of the play was written in Epsom about seven years ago, with only occasional interruptions from an eight-year-old Chinese kid 'fresh off the boat' from Hong Kong who'd just moved in next door. An only child, he was looking for kids to play with, but while Oscar and I were too busy finishing our script to kick a soccer ball around with him, he did give us the idea for the Chinese character who appears in the very last scene of the play.

Niu Sila celebrates the Pacific Island migration to New Zealand that occurred during the 1960s and 70s, as well as the wonderful multicultural nature of many of our older suburbs. In Auckland these were once places like Grey Lynn and Ponsonby, and today are the increasingly culturally diverse areas such as Kingsland and Mount Roskill. It's places like these that make Auckland the perfect setting for *Niu Sila* with it's crazy multicultural cast of over thirty characters (all played by the two actors), including an entire Indian cricket team.

During the 1970s and 80s, I was a frequent visitor to Auckland, and the influence of the world's biggest Polynesian city on me was profound. I often played with bands at the Gluepot tavern. Ponsonby was a great old suburb back then, despite (or because of?) there hardly being a latte in sight. As much as I loved the Gluepot, it was the downstairs bar, with its mix of old Palagi men with their *Best Bets*, and younger Polynesian men with 70s-style Afros that I found fascinating. Then there's South Auckland. The mere mention of the word can stir up fear and loathing amongst white New Zealanders who've never actually bothered to go there and see the place for themselves. But the most interesting South Auckland experiences I had were far from scary, apart from being chased by some gang members in a red Valiant charger, but that was strictly South-East Auckland and it was very late at night.

One evening I landed in Auckland on a delayed flight from Australia. I'd missed the last flight back to Wellington so I was put up in a Mangere hotel within a stone's throw of the airport. Against the advice of the Palagi motelier, I went for a walk and looked into the hall down the road, where a social to raise funds for victims of a recent cyclone in the Pacific was being held. Though I was a total stranger, I was welcomed inside. The only white person there, I had food thrust upon me, cackling old grannies and aunties insisted I dance with them, I fell in love a hundred times with gorgeous Polynesian princesses in stunning floral dresses, and I discovered the wonderful music of Samoan band The Five Stars. Then to end the evening, a young Samoan guy gave me two cans of beer for the 'trip home' to my motel – about 100 metres.

I know a lot of bad stuff goes on in South Auckland, but I'll never forget my night in Mangere, and the friendly generosity of those in that hall. Incidents like this one taught me that Palagi New Zealanders have got to accept that Pacific people bring far more positives to this country than negatives, and that those positives are not just in the clichéd areas of rugby and entertainment.

Next time I was up in Auckland I took my elderly Palagi father-in-law, who lived in Papakura, to the Otara Markets. At first he seemed terrified – 'no one ever goes to Otara round here,' he yelled as I forced him into the back of the car, 'it's full of bloody Islanders.' However, he was a very keen gardener and after inspecting all the amazing taro, bananas, beans, coriander, coconuts, mangoes, papayas on display, and enjoying a very nice cup of koko Samoa, he conceded it was an extremely enjoyable morning after all.

I could go on about the amazing Asian foodhalls one finds around Queen Street, the fascinating mix of cultures one can witness in suburbs like Onehunga, the wonderful theatre and short films coming out of the city's Pacific and Asian communities, and the fascinating mix of languages one notices at the taxi stand at Auckland airport.

As much as I love the Harbour Bridge, the Viaduct Basin, Ponsonby cafes, the Waitakeres, and the acoustics of the Auckland Town Hall, the real jewel in Auckland's crown is its multicultural population. Let's hope all Aucklanders, and eventually all New Zealanders, will come to fully appreciate it.

Setting is more important in some texts than others. In most cases it is valuable to spend some time looking into where the author chose to set their text.

1. Answer the following questions:
   - Where is the text set? (Think cultural as well as geographic.)
   - When is the text set?
   - How are details used to recreate time and place?
   - Is there more than one setting? Are they contrasted?
   - What is the cultural setting, religion, race, gender, class?
   - Does the setting influence the characters' actions in any way i.e. extreme isolation?
2. *Niu Sila* was originally performed in two large cities. It has been said that '*Niu Sila* has been "Auckland-ified" in the shift from the capital. Porirua has become Mangere, Brooklyn is now Ponsonby.' What does this quotation tell you about the setting of the play?
3. For each of the listed places write a description of it using detail from the play.
   - Peter's home
   - Ioane's home
   - Huntington Street (neighbours, etc).
4. At the end of the play Peter says '… I live in a town house in the trendy part of the city, and there's no Islanders around. The only tapa cloth in the street is at the local café – which does a lovely flat white. In fact, the whole neighbourhood's flat and white …' Explain what you think he means by this.
5. To a degree the central city setting of *Niu Sila* no longer exists. When once it was the norm to find a mixture of classes and ethnic groups on one street it is now the norm to categorise whole suburbs by the same system. What have we as a nation lost because of this?

Link to NCEA:

Use the notes you have gathered above to answer ONE of the essay questions below.

1. Describe an **important time or place** in the text. Explain why this time or place is important in the text.

   Tip: *The setting as a whole is multicultural Auckland during the 70's. There are several descriptions in this play that will help you describe this. You can focus your description on the street where Ioane and Peter live as a specific example of this era. The second part of the question asks for you to explain why this is important. Think about relating it to theme.*

2. Describe a **memorable setting** in the text.
   Explain **how** this setting helped you **understand an idea (or ideas)** in the text.

   Tip: *Look at the hints for the question above to help you.*

DRAMA ACTIVITIES

Level 1

Devising drama: (2-3 lessons)

- In groups of 3-4 tell stories about your first day of school OR a moment when you realised you had formed a new friendship OR share a memory of childhood games you played.

Tip: *Share a story you do not mind the whole class hearing.*

- Your group chooses one of the stories they have shared to act out. When choosing the story consider which one has the most dramatic potential.

Tip: *Think about the elements of drama. What features are always present in drama? What elements could drama not exist without (for example, time, space, movement, voice, tension)? Consider how elements are present in the story you have chosen to act out.*

- Decide on 3 key moments from the story. Create 3 freeze-frames (tableaux) to show these 3 key moments. Add sounds but no words at this stage. You will get approximately 5 minutes for preparation. Workshop where necessary to create effective moments of drama. Present to the class.

Tip: *Consider levels, use of space, point of focus (split or single) and try to achieve a sense of unity in the freeze-frame.*

- Now link the 3 key moments using words and movement. Aim for a 2-3 minute story. Take approximately 15-20 minutes for preparation. Present your stories to the class.

- As a class revise conventions (ways of telling a story). List different conventions in your drama journal (for example, flocking, shadowing, cannoning, repetition, slow-motion, freeze-frames and so on).

- Using the list of conventions you have worked on above add two symbolic conventions to the story you have presented. Rework this in your groups and then present your reworked story to the class.

Tip: *It is important to create a symbolic scene rather than making the scene natural.*

Tip: *Choose a moment where you want to increase the tension to add in the convention.*

- As a class discuss the impact adding the conventions made to your stories. Record your discoveries in your drama journal.

Tip: *Switch journals with another class member and share what you discovered while your partner records what you are saying.*

Prepare a role from Niu Sila

- Read through the play as a class. Stand and be as physical as you can while reading, OR
- Divide the class into two groups. While one group reads the play the other group can perform the movement.

After reading the play

- ✻ In small groups, choose a scene from the play. Decide which character you will play and make sure your scene will last approximately 10 minutes.

- ✻ To help you understand and reflect on your role, record ideas for the development of your character in your journal.

- ✻ As a group, re-read the scene you have chosen. In your journal jot down any decisions you will have to make.

- ✻ Answer the following questions about your character in your journal :
  - What are your character's major desires and dislikes?
  - How is your character viewed by other characters in the play?
  - What are your physical characteristics?

- ✻ Hot seat each character in front of the class to consider how deeply you know your role. Make a Role on the Wall for your character. Discuss what you have discovered about your character and the implications this has for your group's final performance.

- ✻ Write a timeline for what you will need to do before the final performance of your scene. Consider production responsibilities, learning lines, rehearsing with your group. Record this in your journal.

- ✻ Rehearse your scene. Block moves and record these stage directions on your script. Record all challenges and decisions made in your journal as you continue through the production process. Remember to use full use of the space available on stage, consider carefully how you are using your voice and movement to create your character.

- ✻ Work together as a group to prepare any props, costume, lighting or music you require for the final performance and rehearse using all these technologies prior to the presentation day. Be prepared to make changes where necessary and record these changes in your journal.

Link to NCEA:

Niu Sila can be used to assess performances in an acting role.

Level 2

Activity 1:

Watch film / TV footage of some Pacific New Zealand productions.

View : *Bro Town*

Sione's Wedding

In your class discuss the nature of stereotypes.
Think about :

- ✻ What is a stereotype? List some.

- ✻ How are the characters in the film / programme you have viewed stereotypical?

- ✻ How are they more than this?

- ✻ What is the impact of performing a character that could be viewed as a stereotype?

Record your responses in your drama journal.

Activity 2:

Read "From Falealilito Ponsonby", an extract from *Polynesian Panthers* edited by Melani Anae with Lautofa (Ta) Iuli and Leilani Burgvne.

In groups of 3-5:

- Draw an outline of a body on a large piece of paper. Get one of your group members to lie on the paper while you trace around them.
- Consider why a person might leave their country to come to New Zealand. You could keep this general or focus specifically on travel from the Pacific Islands. Write your group's ideas in the centre of the figure.
- What features are stereotypically associated with being Pacifica (for example, eats taro, wears floral dresses). Record these features on the outside of the figure.

Activity 3

Read page 42 in *Polynesian Panthers* and pages 60-63 (Panther Twenty-Nine Wayne Toleafoa) for background information on New Zealand in the 1970s.

- In groups devise around individual stories such as "A Boy Called Broke : Part B – Journey to the cells" by Fa'amoana John Luafutu (pages 45-48) and "Interview with Tigilau Ness Tigilau: Ness talks with Lito Vilisoni", National Radio (pages 65-68).
- In the same groups, workshop the individual stories adding one convention at a time. For example, add 5 freeze frames to show the 5 key moments of the story, then add a flash-back (using symbolic use of space), a moment of slow motion, a moment when the audience are addressed and so on.
- After a week or two of workshopping and discussing conventions, work together as a class to put a piece of devised work together about the Dawn Raids.
- You are expected to do your own research on this time period but your teacher can provide computer and library time to do this effectively.
- **OR:** Devise a piece around the Springbok Tour of 1981 to explore New Zealand history and politics.

Activity 4

Read through *Niu Sila* as a class.

- Nominate someone to record any questions or comments that come up as the reading is happening.
- Choose a role that you want to perform and prepare your audition. You may choose to perform a technical or support role so consider what is required for this.
- Block moves. Record stage directions on your script as appropriate.
- As a class, set deadlines for lines to be learnt, production decisions to be made and issue a clear rehearsal schedule.

Tip: *Apply for the rights to perform the play well in advance of your performance dates. These can be purchased through Playmarket (see page 88).*

Link to NCEA:

Niu Sila can be performed (and assessed) as the significant production of the year at NCEA levels 2 or 3.

Level 3

Activity 1

Read the article 'Pacific Arts in New Zealand' by Sean Mallon.

- Get into groups of 3. Break the article into three chunks. One member of your group reads aloud the first section, a second member summarises what has been heard, the third group member writes a question or idea that comes from the material. Repeat this activity for the other two chunks of the article, swapping roles to do so.

Activity 2

Listen to music from CD *Conscious Roots 2*. (*Frisk Me Down* by Katchafire and *Meaning of Life* by Toki both have strong political messages and are good starting points)

- Write the key points or messages that you pick up from the music in your drama journal.
- Using the resources from Activities 1 and 2, discuss the purpose of arts as a form of expression. You could choose to look at visual arts / music / dance / drama to explore the importance of expressing a viewpoint.

Tip: *It is useful to stress the political messages that are carried in artistic forms. This creates a stronger response to the theatre form question in the exam.*

Activity 3

* In small groups (2-3) choose one Pacific New Zealand play written between 1990-2007 (the the list of resources on page 88). Read this play together and research
  - the playwright
  - the social / political history of this play (for example, what happening in New Zealand and the Pacific when this play was written and/or set).
  - the story and characters
  - stylistic notes about the production.
* Present this information to the class in a clear and interesting way.
* Take notes in your journal about each play as you listen to the other presentations.
* You should read at least five of the plays from the genre of Pacific theatre in New Zealand.
* After all the presentations discuss and note common features of Pacific theatre in New Zealand. Record these features in your drama journal.

Activity 4

* Read the chapter titled 'Taking Centre Stage: Pacific Theatre in New Zealand' written by Anton Carter from *Pacific Arts Niu Sila – Contemporary New Zealand Arts* by Sean Mallon and Pandora Fulimalo Pereira, Te Papa Press, Wellington, 2002.
* Refine or add to the list of features of Pacific theatre in New Zealand.

Activity 5

* As a class view the documentary: *Chinks, Coconuts and Curry-Munchers*, Kiwa Productions, TV3, 2002. (Available for purchase from Kiwa Productions.)
* Discuss the nature and power of stereotypes. Think about:
  - Why are stereotypes used in theatre/film/television?
  - How are they linked to politics? What political message do they contain?
  - What damage can use of stereotypes do?
  - How can they be helpful?

Activity 6

* You may choose to do some devising work before reading the play *Niu Sila*. This could be around the idea of friendship as suggested in the activity for Level 1 or you could research and prepare work around the Dawn Raids or Springbok Tour (see activities for Level 2).

Activity 7

Niu Sila can be performed (and assessed) as the significant production of the year at NCEA levels 2 or 3.

* Prepare and perform the play (refer to notes under Level 2).

Tip: *Refer to specific task instructions on tki website for 3.5 (Achievement Standard 90611)* Research and carry out a performance or technical/production role in a significant production – *6 Credits – internal.*

Tip: *The student instructions must be written specifically for your production of* Niu Sila. *Adapt the task and get approval from the National Drama Advisors for your area. Make sure you are looking at the latest version of the task and assessment criteria (check the NZQA website for latest version).*

Link to NCEA:

At this level it is important for you to view the play in a wider social and political context. *Niu Sila* can be used as part of a wider study on Pacific Theatre in New Zealand. This can be treated as a theatre form and used for assessment in the external exam. *Niu Sila* can be defined as part of any theatre form you choose providing it has features which can be clearly identified.

To make this task easier define the theatre form specifically, for example, choose to look at Pacific Theatre in New Zealand from 1990-2007.

The play can be performed (and assessed) as the significant production of the

Resources

Film / TV

No. 2, directed by Toa Fraser, Colonial Encounters & Southern Light Films, 2006.

Sione's Wedding,directed by Chris Graeme, South Pacific Pictures, 2006.

Bro Town, Firehorse Films, 2006.

Chinks, Coconuts and Curry-Munchers, Kiwa Productions, TV3, 2002.

Books

Pacific Art Niu Sila – Contemporary New Zealand Arts, by Sean Mallon and Pandora Fulimalo Pereira, Te Papa Press, Wellington, 2002.

Polynesian Panthers, edited by Melani Anae with Lautofa (Ta) Iuli and Leilani Burgvne, Reed Publishing (NZ) Ltd, Auckland, 2006.

Articles / Resources online

Pacific Arts in New Zealand by Sean Mallon, http://www.creativenzgovt.nz/resources/Pacific-arts.pdf , 2001.

Niu Sila ATC Education Unit Teacher's Pack, Phttp://www.atc.co.nz/PDFs/Education_TeachersPack_NiuSila.pdf

Plays (all available from Playmarket)

Bare, by Toa Fraser, 1998

No.2, By Toa Fraser, 1999

Paradise, by Toa Fraser, 2000

Think of a Garden, by John Kneubuhl

Sons, by Victor Rodger, 1995

Mapaki, by Diana Fuemana, 2004

Fresh off the Boat, by Oscar Kightley and Simon Small, 1993

A Frigate Bird Sings, by Oscar Kightley and Dave Fane, 1996

Dawn Raids, by Oscar Kightley, 1997

Frangipani Perfume, by Makerita Urale, 2004

The Songmaker's Chair, by Albert Wendt, 2004

Music

Conscious Roots 2, Capitol Music, 2005.

Contact details of organisations

Playmarket, P.O. Box 9767, Te Aro, Wellington.
Phone : 04 382 8462. Email : info@playmarket.org.nz

Kiwa Production http://www.kiwaproductions.co.nz/enquire.php